LAUNCHED

ROB FEINSTEIN

This book is dedicated with love to my wife, Tara, who taught me that all dreams are possible when you don't resist them.

**START YOUR CAREER
RIGHT AFTER COLLEGE
EVEN DURING A PANDEMIC**

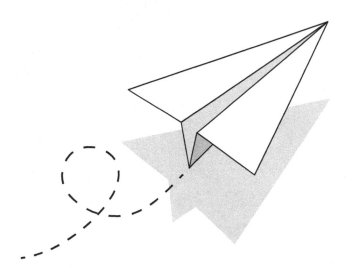

LAUNCHED

ROB FEINSTEIN

CONTENTS

*The secret to getting ahead
is getting started.*

MARK TWAIN

PREFACE

A NEW ABNORMAL

This book's system is timeless, but its timing is not.

As I write this, it is the summer of 2020 and the world is ensnared by the Covid-19 pandemic. I'm looking for a good piece of wood to knock on while I contemplate being thankful for my family's good health to this point. But the world outside is turbulent, to say the least. The pandemic has changed everything, and it's unclear at this moment when, if and even how it may abate.

Amidst the global devastation in deaths, sickness and fear—and an empathetic concern for others whose fate has been worse than our own—it's fair to consider a few simple questions as a college student or new college graduate: "What will this mean to me?" and "How will my career get started now?"

That's not selfish or petty. It's realistic and practical.

In the years leading up to 2020, it was easy for college students to feel confident about life after graduation. The longest economic expansion in U.S. history heralded record-low unemployment and a humming entry-level job market. You may have had well-laid plans to start your career, or felt that considering your early career choices could be safely delayed until it was time to get your first job after graduation.

But as the coronavirus swept the world, the flywheel of college students entering the workforce quickly busted. According to Glassdoor, more than half of 2020's summer internships were cancelled. Most of the remaining ones turned virtual—often offering far less valuable experiences than originally planned. Countless other jobs were lost. Those impacted now know the feelings and fears of an experience gap that's easy to explain but hard to stomach. That lost opportunity has its cost, and its effects will be felt for years to come. Looking forward, you may be feeling a sharp pinch of anxiety as you consider your job prospects after college. You're left to regroup and focus on looking for new ways to regain momentum and successfully launch your career.

But fear not.

If you're graduating, or have already graduated, and you're trying to figure out how to get your career off the ground, this book will help.

If you're still early in your college career and you want a career foundation game plan for your remaining years as a student, this book will help.

If you haven't figured out what you want to do for a career when you're out of college, this book will help.

If you were so busy working at any job you could find just to pay for college, and wonder how that experience translates to your chosen career, this book will help.

Why should you believe me?

For one, I'm a pioneer in the online recruiting industry. I have an insider's perspective on how hiring really works and the technology that drives it. I was an executive at CareerPath, a consortium of newspaper publishers who combined their employment advertising into what at the time was the world's largest online jobs database. Under my direction, CareerPath also developed groundbreaking online recruitment tools including one of the Web's largest and deeply searchable resume databases. Later, I ran MonsterTRAK, the new-college-grad arm of the job listings giant Monster.com, which developed the software that major employers and college career centers used to manage hiring of tens of thousands of students annually.

I also know hiring from the perspective of more than 25 years as a technology industry leader. I've sat on the other side of the table from job candidates of all levels of experience—from college students seeking internships to prospective chief executives. I've interviewed and hired hundreds of professionals, so I know intimately how recruiting is done in the real world.

With the benefit of that experience, let me share a little secret that many of us in the hiring world know, but few will say: college students and new college grads aren't very good at presenting themselves to the full-time job market.

Sure, there are candidates who perform impressively well. But I've also witnessed with dismay that most candidates fail to execute the most obvious and simple strategies to stand out, be noticed and get hired. It has always surprised and saddened me that altogether too commonly, candidates aren't prepared to perform well enough in an interview setting to get a job. Further, most young candidates aren't adept at describing how their limited work and life experiences translate to marketable job skills.

Truth is, it's not that hard to do with a little guidance and practice—even in this era of significant uncertainty.

I wrote this book as a guide that's especially important in this time of change. It's a step-by-step system to develop the skills that will be relevant to launching your career after college—no matter what challenges the new environment may bring. We are all living in a 'new abnormal', and there is indeed ground to make up. But this book will help you to regain some needed traction in order to effectively package and market yourself to get launched.

Most of the lessons are evergreen. They teach you how to employ the standard tactics of succeeding as a high-ceiling professional prospect, and the things that most job candidates don't do anywhere near as well as they should. I'll share a framework to help you choose a career you'll love. I'll teach you how to master the craft of identifying and securing a job to start your career. You'll learn to better prepare for interviews, construct a distinctly compelling resume, and how to present yourself as the uniquely interesting person you are. You'll emerge with better tools than most professionals have at any level of their careers—not just students and new grads.

Still, the standard tactics need some updating to fit a Covid-era career search. The pandemic has changed the rules of the game—in many ways, most likely, forever. Working from home and remote job searching are now the norm—requiring a new set of skills to master. As a college student planning the start of your career, or a recent graduate navigating this shifted landscape, you'll need new levels of creativity to find work, gain experience and present yourself successfully to prospective employers. You may even need to change your intended career path if you've been targeting an industry especially shaken by the pandemic, such as retail, travel, entertainment or commercial real estate.

"We're moving away from a time when the question has been 'Who do you want to be, what do you want to become,' to 'How do you get a job and participate in the economy so you can support yourself,'" said Kelley Bishop, who heads the career center at the University of Maryland, and previously held similar roles at Michigan State and Syracuse University. "When you do that, the needle starts to move back to the pragmatic."

Or as Scott Williams, longtime executive director of the career center at the University of Georgia, put it, "I think it's just going to create a more competitive job market. Students are going to have to have that Plan B, and maybe that Plan C, in mind. I don't think students thought about that as much over the last five years."

How will you be competitive?

The most obvious form of experience, of course, is in jobs—via one or more internships or other work experiences during college or immediately thereafter. There's no doubt that's the best type of experience to have entering the workforce. Internships show employers that you're focused, driven and that you're acting on your career vision. Jobs—no matter the work you're being paid to do—show employers that you're responsible, mature and know how to contribute in a workplace. If you have good work experience, then you're starting the race with a lead. Your next challenge is to learn how to leverage that experience to your best advantage. This book will teach you how.

But what if you haven't had much work experience, or haven't had the opportunity for internships? If that's you, then you can still get back in the race.

It's critical to recognize that the experiences employers value aren't limited to only those you gain in a job. The key to being attractive to employers is to create a compelling narrative about yourself based on all your accumulated life experiences. For example, you may have gained project management experience in volunteer activities, gotten leadership experience in school projects, or learned how to overcome adversity and strive for improvement as an athlete. These are all skills that employers value. This book will help you communicate all your relevant experiences as valued workplace skills, and to develop your unique story.

The keys, in good and troubled times alike, are to stay active, test the bounds of your comfort zone, and never stop accumulating experiences. That's the path to winning, and one where you can be in control even when the job market is tight. The winners will adapt and be more creative. To be one of the winners, you'll need to learn to improve yourself virtually—through tactics such as online learning, self-teaching, and crafting experiences on your own to develop a portfolio of your work. You'll need to be more proactive and strategic about how you choose a career path, how you prepare yourself for it, and how to assure that you'll get maximum value from internships, jobs and other experiences. It's a different world that requires a refined approach to career management for students in their college years and those seeking their first jobs after graduation.

Employers will not simply accept as fate that the pandemic has slowed you down. Surely, they will understand the challenges. But they will be looking for how you overcame them. The most popular interview question over the next few years will be: "What did you do during the pandemic?"

While the full, longstanding impact of Covid-19 is not yet known, one thing is certain. We have dug a hole, and we don't yet know how deep it will be or how long it will take to climb out. In the near term, at minimum, we all must adjust.

"I'm really going to be eager to see what happens now that we've gone from having one of the most delightful job markets any college graduate could wish for to now you're back to what a lot of other generations have faced in hardship," Bishop told me.

How we got here

The virus isn't all that's to blame, though. In many ways, the pre-pandemic boom masked significant underlying issues. Long-simmering trends were brought to a boil—gallons of demographic and attitudinal shifts that had already begun to reshape the entry-level job market. It's not your parents' era anymore. It's not the backdrop they knew when they were at the same point in their lives.

Multiple factors are at play. For one, there are far more college graduates than there used to be—ever. Only about one-third of college-age people were in college in 1980, and today it's more than half, according to the U.S. Census Bureau. That's a huge shift, and it's had a profound impact. A college degree used to be a distinguishing credential—a professional entry ticket in itself. College graduates were special snowflakes. But we're not living in that world anymore. A college degree alone—even from an elite university—isn't anywhere near the differentiator it was a generation ago. And with calls in some circles to make a college education free to all who seek it, those figures could be driven even higher, which would further dilute the distinctive value that a college education once provided.

The harsh reality is that college grads need far more than a degree to be competitive in today's job market. Internships are now like the t-shirt with your school's name on it; nearly every student has one. Not only is it assumed that you'll have some amount of professional experience before your first full-time job, but the new norm is for students to have multiple internships and other workplace experiences by the time they graduate. Some campuses report that 80% or more of their students have had at least one internship before graduating, and often have two or more internships. And while unheard of even a few years ago, it's now accepted that in ultra-competitive industries—fashion is an example—even new graduates are still offered internships instead of full-time roles as a proving ground.

Making things worse, employers have been complaining to colleges in recent years that graduates are in fact not as prepared to enter the workforce as they need to be. Employers have been underwhelmed for a while by college students' readiness for workplace success. This long-festering disillusionment, once a whispered concern, is now loudly in the conversation.

The flash point was a 2019 survey that measured just how miffed employers are by how under-prepared new college grads are to function well at work. The study measured student and employer perception of new grads' career readiness based on a set of specific competencies required for workplace success. Students scored most poorly in the employers' eyes on leadership, intercultural fluency and career management. The biggest gaps in proficiency ratings—the ones where students' perception of their own skills were much grander than employers' perception of students—were in professionalism, leadership, communication and career management. That's a pretty damning disconnect. Employers are simply not as impressed with new grads as new grads are with themselves.

CAREER COMPETENCIES

Teamwork	Professionalism	Communication	Leadership
Intercultural Fluency	Digital Technology	Problem Solving	Career Management

Source: National Association of Colleges and Employers

The coronavirus pandemic and its wake exacerbate all these underlying trends. Its impact adds salt—and a dash of hot pepper, too—to already-inflicted wounds. It's heightened the need to craft a strategy to stand out in the competitive job market. Add it all together—a tightened job market, underlying issues of too many students being under-prepared, and havoc to the economy from the pandemic—and the challenges facing new college graduates are more daunting than ever. A solid foundation—including internships, work and other experiences—is now the de facto baseline. Standing out requires more.

The environment for today's college students and new college grads is more competitive than ever. Today's college students are best served to have an after-college strategy that's formulated and executed starting early in their college years. But regardless of when you get started—even if it's after you've graduated—you need a plan to accumulate a set of skills and experiences to make yourself marketable in the working world.

Parents have a role, too. They must educate themselves on the realities of today's job market to be effective cheerleaders and sources of currently applicable wisdom. Recognize that the juncture from college to career is often fraught with pressure, anxiety and doubt—some of which parents may admit in reflective moments that they themselves have caused. The lessons in this book will help parents to be productively engaged in the process.

As a student or new graduate, the references to 'you' in this book apply to you. Yes, you. Unlike your parents when they started out, you're not being asked to make a 40-year commitment—or more—to a narrow career path or a supposedly stable single employer that you'll be tethered to for a lifetime. That may have been a realistic expectation when your parents entered the workforce, but it's certainly not pragmatic today. Your generation is likely to have far more careers in your professional lives than your parents did in their day. Still, the better you get at picking your initial path, the more ably you'll navigate the changes you'll make in career choices throughout your life.

Good luck! This book is here to help.

CHAPTER 1

THE SYSTEM

Debbie was ready to celebrate.

She was waiting to meet her son, Brad, at the iconic and tony Polo Lounge at the Beverly Hills Hotel, known as much for its bubble-gum pink tablecloths as being a top see-and-be-seen fish bowl for Hollywood stars and dealmakers. To L.A. locals, the Polo Lounge is also a go-to for special family events: milestone birthdays and anniversaries, graduations and the like. At $23 per cocktail, it's not just for any old happy hour.

This was indeed expected to be a special, happy occasion. Brad, a college senior, was to be feted for getting his first job—or so they both thought. But when Brad arrived a few minutes late, his face flushed and his cheeks damp from brushed-away tears, Debbie knew this would be no victory party.

What had happened? It was all set up perfectly, Debbie thought. Her husband, Quinn, a longtime television and commercials actor, had called in a favor from a former agent and gotten Brad an interview at a Hollywood talent agency. She had thought: wasn't that 'in' enough to get Brad hired, rendering the interview a mere formality? Unsurprisingly to me, no, it was not.

Brad soon composed himself. Maybe those pink tablecloths were chosen for their soothing effects, helping to soften the blow of actors and actresses receiving bad news from their agents since Hollywood's early days. Brad told Debbie how terribly his meeting had gone. The interviewer, an executive at the agency, was friendly enough. But he caught Brad off guard with some standard interview questions. Why was Brad interested in working at an agency, and why this agency in particular? What were his career aspirations? What in Brad's experiences translated to the demanding work of a Hollywood talent agency? Brad felt gut-punched. He wasn't prepared to answer any of these questions. The interview was excruciating. His prospects for this job, it appeared certain, had been lost. And so had the joy of this visit to the Polo Lounge.

That night, Debbie called me to ask if I could help. Our families have been close friends ever since our kids were toddlers. It wasn't an unexpected call. For families we know, I'm the one frequently asked to help with their kids' career planning. I was happy to help out Brad in any way I could.

We met a few days later, and he told me everything that Debbie had recounted to me earlier, and more. Tellingly, he described his limited resume. He had precious little work experience, no internships, and no significant activities on campus. That's why I've changed the names of Brad and his parents in telling this story. Still, the things Brad had to learn were not that different from many students I've met over the years.

Brad's intentions were good, but in our conversation he meandered. He didn't provide me with any kind of clear summary of the person he had become or what would make him appealing as a contributor in any organization—let alone the talent agency. So I raised my hand to gently stop him.

"What you need to understand," I told him, "is that getting a job is a marketing exercise, and you're the product being marketed."

He looked at me quizzically, so I explained the metaphor. Just like any product, there's a buyer and a seller. In the case of a career, the buyer is the employer and candidates are selling themselves as the product. As with any product, it sells only when its distinctiveness is clear, and its benefits fulfill an acknowledged need. Great products have features that buyers already know they want—or features that buyers can be coaxed into realizing they want—and whose benefits are quickly appreciated when explained well. Products need to have all the right attributes, and be marketed well, to succeed in the marketplace—just like a job candidate in the employment market. Brad needed to understand that getting an introduction to the talent agency executive was a great start—an excellent example of first-class networking, albeit from the advantaged perch of a family connection that most students can only dream of—but it was only a first step toward actually getting the job. He hadn't yet sold the product—himself—or considered how to achieve that.

In my own career in software, I've spent most of my time in a function called product management. That means it's been my job to identify business opportunities for new software, and new features added to existing software, that specific types of users want and need. In that world, success is achieved when your target user sees your software as a solution to a problem that matters to them. It needs to be extremely easy for the user to understand the issue you're addressing, why it's significant enough that it demands an immediate solution, and why your software is the perfect salve to take their pain away. Sound familiar? This is exactly what you're trying to do in thinking of yourself as a product that needs to be marketed well to be successful.

I've launched dozens of software products and their enhancements in my business career, including several in the online recruitment space. It's clear to me that too many job candidates—of all ages, not just college students and those just starting their careers—sell themselves short in interview settings. They've got plenty to offer, but the impression they unwittingly leave is that they're bad products: poorly positioned, ill marketed and ultimately—to me, anyway—they don't get sold. And 'sold' to a job candidate means getting hired. In sum, they're the worst combination of all: they're not necessarily bad products, they're just poorly marketed. They lack an easy-to-execute plan to tell a story, stand out from the field, and be recognized for the irresistible new hire they could be.

That plan is easier to execute when you wrap your head around the notion that you're the product. Don't worry. I'm not trying to turn you into some random item you can purchase on Amazon with one click. But I absolutely do want you to get comfortable with thinking of yourself as a product. It's actually an affirming and humanizing part of a healthy self-image, because it focuses your mind on what makes you different, special and worthy. It's also a necessary and practical exercise in a job search. It helps you crystallize, in the eyes of any potential employer, why you're the best and only right fit for the job opening they want to fill. It answers the employer's most important question: why you?

Think of the last time you purchased something. Maybe you bought new pants at your favorite clothing store, or got a new cell phone. Odds are you made a choice from among several options, based on something that just clicked with you. The pants may have been perfect for a party that was coming up. The cell phone might have just the right camera for the kind of photos you want to share with your friends. One way or the other, it was clear to you that the items you chose had what you wanted. And you pulled out your credit card to buy.

That's just what employers do when they consider you for a job opening. They're choosing from their own merchandise aisle of options: the others who are applying for the same position as you are. Each employer has a set of attributes in mind for what kind of person will be the right fit for their open role. Some people they meet will seem to be obvious fits, and others might be great 'square pegs' but poor fits for the 'round hole' of the job opening they're trying to fill. Someone will get an offer, while the others will keep looking. Often it should be you, but it won't be if you don't do a good job of positioning yourself compellingly in the eyes of a hiring manager or recruiter.

When you craft your career plan and think of yourself as a product, it permeates every bit of your thinking. That includes the experiences you've had and how you describe them, which internships or other jobs and activities you seek out to bolster your resume during your college years, how you construct your resume and social profiles, how you compose a cover letter, and how you develop a game plan for an interview. It prepares you to fulfill your passions in a career, not just get any old job. How you package and present yourself impacts the decision to hire you—just like any other product and its buyers' decisions to purchase or not.

With Brad, I touched on a few of the many recommendations that are described in detail in this book. Brad needed help crafting a narrative about his life that created a sense of direction—a near inevitability—that pointed him toward agency work. He needed to learn more about the agency before entering the interview, so he could ask questions to showcase his interest and fit. It's all part of a system I've developed and evolved via countless interactions with young people preparing to start their post-college careers.

Closest to home, I coached my son, Graydon, on all these techniques. With his desired career path to enter the world of luxury goods marketing, Graydon networked his way to an internship at fashion brand Marc Jacobs while an NYU undergrad. He then parlayed that opportunity into other internships at Cartier, Giorgio Armani, and a boutique luxury goods marketing agency. Upon graduation, he landed a full-time role by joining the marketing team for the Americas at Gucci—one of the world's top luxury brands. Now he's using some of the same techniques as he prepares himself for a career shift into interior design. So I know firsthand, and as a proud dad, that these methods work.

In truth, Brad had started thinking about his career way too late. He would have been well-served to have had a four-year game plan for college that included career-related activities along with his academic and other on-campus experiences—as a complement to having fun and enjoying the college experience. Starting during his freshman year, he should have familiarized himself with his campus career center, and started attending events hosted by companies that recruit graduates from his school. He should have gained an evolving understanding of what graduates of his school ended up doing to start their careers, and begun the mental exercise of figuring out which of those paths could be a fit for him. He should have picked campus activities that would engage his passions and broaden his interests, and also given him an opportunity to hone non-academic career skills such as leadership, problem-solving and conflict resolution. In sum, he should have accumulated a set of experiences—and a practiced way of describing them—so that he would have crushed his meeting at the talent agency with ease.

But given that he hadn't done much—if any—of that, I focused Brad in that first session on the tactical approach to how he should have readied himself for his interview at the agency. I shared my easy-to-execute routine to prepare for any interview in only 30 minutes or less. I coached him on a unique method I created to strategically craft questions to ask the interviewer, which not only scores extra points, but also provides a helpful mental break in an otherwise draining interview setting. I molded the tactics specifically to Brad, and to the talent agency opportunity in particular. You'll read more on each of those in later chapters in this book.

Every time I talk about these strategies, as well as the many others I recommend or have developed myself, I feel a touch of melancholy. I'm reminded that so few job candidates in all my years of interviewing have properly prepared for their interviews—or they certainly haven't prepared as well as they could have. They fail to research the company or critically read the job description they're meeting about, and they can't describe themselves compellingly. They either don't have questions ready for me at all, or ask boring questions that miss an opportunity to impress me further. Even if they have some work experience, or activities and experiences that signal some of the qualities I'm looking for—such as leadership, problem-solving and conflict resolution—they don't assemble them into a strong pitch for why they're a great hire for the job at hand.

When I interview candidates, I have a mental habit of imagining my car's gas tank meter hovering over the shoulder of the person I'm interviewing. This make-believe meter moves toward Full or Empty depending on how the interview is going. It wasn't something I consciously decided to do. Rather, it simply appeared one day during an interview, and made its own habit to appear again in almost every interview since then. Too often, it registers toward Empty through most of the session.

The reason so many interviews run on fumes is simple. For all the reasons I've described, too many college students lack the necessary foundation and career management skills to launch their careers seamlessly upon graduation. New college graduates—and the parents who love and nurture them—need a better guide to how to succeed in today's ultra-competitive market for entry-level jobs. The keys to how to do it are contained in this book and described in detail in later chapters. In sum, what you need to do is gather a set of experiences—in school, at work, and in your activities—that you can describe in a way makes you a compelling professional career candidate. It's my goal in this book to bring those skills to all of you.

Good news: Brad's story has a happy ending. He had chances for other jobs, as everyone does. He figured out how to prepare, mostly from practice and hearing 'no' enough times to learn to prepare even more. Ultimately, he entered interviews ready to answer questions—both those he anticipated and those that required thinking on the fly. He was able to steer the conversation to the talking points he wanted to discuss. And finally, he aced an interview and accepted an offer to join a talent firm as an agent's assistant.

Career launched! Now let's get your career launched, too.

CHAPTER 2

GOALS AND OBJECTIVES

No mission can be considered a success unless it has achieved a set of clear, pre-set objectives. Without goals, how can you certify a favorable outcome? So when setting out to launch your career, you have to answer a simple question first: launch what?

For many of you, that's easy and straightforward. You've been planning for years with a specific objective in mind. You're a future doctor or lawyer or Wall Street guru, and that's been core to your self-image for years. For others of you, though, it's non-trivial to figure out what career to pursue. What do you want to do? You're not just looking for any job. Instead, you're seeking to begin a career that's a great match for your talents and interests. You may not have such a clear goal in mind, so for you there's some significant introspection that's required to set an early career objective that will make you fulfilled, financially comfortable, and happy. If you fit into that category, you may find the thought of pinning down your career objective to be daunting. You might be thinking: how can I point myself toward a career when I don't even know what I want to do? It's a fair question.

Whether you've had a plan, or haven't yet formed one, the course isn't always clear, and the path often changes. Michael, a very good friend of mine since childhood, began his college career at Cornell University with a conviction that he was a future engineer. He was committed to it. In fact, he'd grown up with it. Michael's father was a creative and enterprising electrical engineer with several groundbreaking accomplishments in television technology, including the development of some of the first special effects for televised sports coverage. Michael was a silicon chip off the block, with natural gifts for engineering, and he secured a summer internship during college working alongside electrical engineers near Boston at one of the world's largest computer manufacturing companies. But that's where his assumed life plan started to wobble. Michael just wasn't motivated by the work, and he couldn't picture himself with the life of his colleagues in the engineering lab—hunched over their desks most of the day, deep in concentration. It just wasn't for him, and it took a summer internship experience to learn that about himself. So Michael re-geared, applied to law school, and began a career in public policy—a fulfilling journey that he's still pursuing. Pivot and re-launch: successful.

The idea of college as a foundation for career is already firmly in place for students in some disciplines. There have always been more pre-professional college majors with clear career paths, such as accounting majors going into accounting careers, or engineering and computer science majors moving seamlessly into jobs in those fields—just like Michael thought he would. In many ways, it's easier for the accounting and engineering majors. For them, the trail is made clear to follow from their first steps on campus. Their coursework is geared toward the practical, and it's easy to make the connection between what they're studying in school and what they'll be trained for and will recognize when on the job. Often, the skills taught in school match the tasks to be done at work. Major companies frequently participate in school projects as a means to influence curriculum and expose students hands-on to their companies.

Life is different for the poets on the liberal arts side of campus. For English and Philosophy majors, and their ilk, the link of their cerebral studies to career is less clear. In many academics' eyes, practical considerations are considered beside the point of training one's mind to think. I believe there's merit to a liberal arts education. I was a history major myself. It's a wonderful path to a fulfilling life. But I also embrace the reality that finding a fulfilling livelihood is a critical component of a well-lived life, too. Still, it's inescapable that the connection from coursework to career is far less clear for liberal arts majors than their engineer and accountant friends. So it requires far more thought and input to set their career foundations while also pursuing a classical education.

The University of Maryland's Bishop lived the liberal arts enigma himself as an undergraduate English major at Dartmouth. "Shakespeare is filled with insights on human dynamics, the frailty of organizations, and so much more," he told me. "I can think of all the things that were transferable out of that even though I can't remember any of the stuff that would have gotten me into a doctoral program about the content itself. Connecting the dots is more difficult for some students than others. If I want to be a doctor, or a computer scientist, there's a curriculum for that. If I'm an English major, my path is only evident after the fact."

Perhaps in response to this ambiguity in college-to-career connections, students are opting for liberal arts majors far less frequently than in the past. A recent study sponsored by the American Enterprise Institute found that students graduating with English and History majors dropped 22-25 percent from 2007 to 2016, while the STEM majors (science, technology, engineering and math) showed enormous gains during the same period. "Schools must offer more opportunities for students to build in-demand skills through strategic curriculum development, the development of work-based learning opportunities such as internships or co-ops, and stronger ties with local employers," the study concluded.

To answer the call for greater hire-ability of college graduates, pre-professional tracks are proliferating. For example, the University of Alabama has a Sales program, the University of Missouri has a degree program in financial planning, and more academic programs now have required internships, practical experiences and corporate-sponsored elements as part of the curriculum. Even the History, Political Science, English and Philosophy professors are being asked to augment their classic approaches with more real-world applications embedded into their teaching. In sum, the pendulum is swinging toward colleges getting more practical and career focused, and this trend will undoubtedly continue.

Whether you've majored in the liberal arts, or you're an engineer or accountant in college, you owe yourself some soul-searching to find or re-confirm your path. You may be on precisely the right path, or you might be more like my friend Michael who needed to reassess what he wanted to do. Personal growth could be described as an evolving understanding, both of yourself and the world around you, based on your accumulation of experiences. Particularly during the college years, when all that is accelerated, it's critical to repeatedly check your assumptions about yourself. Is the path that you're on still the best one for you, based on what you've learned about yourself during this period of rapid personal growth? Only you, through your own self-analysis and reflection, can know the answer for yourself. Many of your likes, dislikes, motivations, and fears are already set inside you; you just need to think about what they are and how they help you decide on a career. Others will only become known as you pursue your career and adjust it as you move through your life. Keep an open mind, follow your inner dialogue, and get your family, friends and career center people involved in the discussion with you.

Finding Your Path

So what do you want to do?

There's a wonderful Japanese concept that relates to finding a purpose and meaning in one's life. It's called *ikigai* (pronounced EE-key-guy) and it's a realistic yet helpfully self-actualizing framework for having a job in the real world that captures your true essence—and therefore creates a greater chance at happiness and success by any definition. *Ikigai* is a rich concept. It accounts for the requirement to have a livelihood, but it also calls for making that work fulfilling, and not just a job. Whether you find yourself with clear direction—on the path to being a doctor, an architect or perhaps a social worker—or still searching, you owe yourself the chance to truly find your *ikigai*.

Ikigai puts this together in a construct that's simple to understand, but will still take some reflection to find its application to your life. You'll need to find the forces that drive you. You'll identify the things that—in a quiet, and self-examining moment—you'll admit you're probably better at than most of your peers. And you need to suss out the parts of you that the world values enough to realistically want to pay you for it.

As the diagram above shows, your *ikigai* is a confluence of four major drivers: what you're good at and what you love, and where that intersects with what the world needs and values enough to sustain your livelihood. The intersections of each allow you to find your passion and mission that's wrapped in a profession that's valued. It's simple, but powerful when you sit down to work out your *ikigai* for yourself.

What is your *ikigai*? Only you can tell. But you need all its aspects in sufficient measure that you can be fulfilled. You get to enjoy your career. It's your opportunity to employ your natural gifts of what you're good at. You get to provide something the world needs, and you get to be paid for it to support the lifestyle you want. Finding your *ikigai* is an exploration, and in a rich life that journey lasts a lifetime of finding new things to enjoy, explore and create.

Your job, of course, is to find your *ikigai* for right now. You need to pick a path for the immediate future, not the next 40 years. It's often difficult to wrap your head around the idea of what you will do professionally for a lifetime. But most people today have multiple careers in their professional lives anyway. A career is a long time, so it should be fulfilling and a match for you at each stage of your professional life, and your *ikigai* may be quite different at various points in your life. It must also pay the bills for the lifestyle you want to achieve.

I encourage you to make the search for your *ikigai* a sharing exercise—one that you engage with family, friends and others who know you well. Sometimes our view of ourselves is skewed when compared to what others see. We can tend to be too hard on ourselves, or unimpressed by things that come to us easily. But in talking to others, you'll be able to gauge your impressions of yourself vs. what others think of you. You may be surprised by the common themes in what people see in your distinctive strengths, as compared to what you see in yourself. Sometimes glass is better than a mirror.

The best way to find your *ikigai* is similar to other tough puzzles to solve: break it down into pieces, and try multiple entry points to get started. Like a jigsaw puzzle, find the edges first and fill in elements of the center as you work through the overall solution. You might find that you are attracted to particular industries, like entertainment, software, or investments. You might be drawn to a particular type of role, such as finance, sales, or engineering. You might have particular skills that you know some people use to make a living, such as design, writing, or problem-solving. Or you may just like certain types of feelings about the work you do, such as helping people, organizing the work of a team, creating something new, or digging into a topic via research. These are all great clues to finding your *ikigai*. Write them down for each of the four outer-most interlocking circles of the *ikigai* diagram. Just as the circles intersect, you're looking for themes that intersect across the circles. For example, what is it that you love that the world needs, and then what of those are you really good at and can be paid for? The more you work at your *ikigai*, the more a pattern of potentially fulfilling career paths will emerge, and the better you'll be at finding a career you'll excel at and enjoy.

Be specific in what you write down about your *ikigai*. Not just shorthand, but complete thoughts that answer 'why' you're passionate about something, and what experiences you've had that proved to you that you're more skilled at something than most of your peers. The detail you add to this personal inventorying will not only help you be more precise in the *ikigai* you build for yourself, but it builds a self-awareness that will enable you to answer questions more crisply when it's time for interviews.

"My advice has always been to think about some stories from your life and experience that can demonstrate who you are," said Kaitlin Greene, who heads internship recruitment for much of the Midwest and Southeast at Northwestern Mutual, which hires thousands of interns and new college grads annually.

Beyond *Ikigai*

To complement your own explorations to find your *ikigai*, your school has other resources in its career center to help you focus on career paths that are a match for you. Allow yourself the opportunity to explore without the burden of whatever preconceived career ideas you may have had. With an open mind, you'll either confirm those plans or find something new. You will also find clues in some diagnostic assessments that your Career Center can guide you toward. Assessments like this aren't a magic potion, so they most likely won't guide you to the perfect career choice in a vacuum. But in the context of other inputs, they can be very helpful.

Different schools, and probably different individual counselors, have their favorites when it comes to assessment tools. The University of Georgia's Williams told me he favors the Strong Interest Inventory—a classic test that typically takes less than an hour but provides insight into the types of occupations and functions for which you're best suited. At the University of Maryland, Bishop's team most commonly administers a different assessment called the Strengths Finder Instrument, which identifies your top areas of strength among a few dozen possibilities. "The idea is that you're going to be more impactful in the world by perfecting what you're good at instead of constantly focusing on what you're not as good at, and at best could be adequate at. So the idea is going with your strengths," Bishop said.

Any assessment tool's impact, though, comes in its connection to other inputs: what you already know about yourself, what you learn about yourself through classroom, work and other activities, and your own gut. By combining all those inputs thoughtfully, "that's where the Ah-hah's come," Bishop told me. "Assessments are good at awakening something."

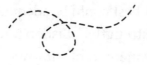

CHAPTER 2 EXERCISES

☐ Do your own *ikigai* exercise, and involve others in the process. Write down your conclusions and be sure to save the results to reflect on your conclusions and be mindful of any changes based on new experiences.

☐ Visit your campus career center and take one of the assessments they recommend. Or find one online that you can take for free or under $20 at sites like self-directed-search.com, mynextmove.org, strengthsquest.com, or myplan.com. Most assessments are either free or very low cost. Make an appointment with your career center to review the results and get their insights.

CHAPTER 3

GATHERING EXPERIENCES

I love straight lines. They're direct and purposeful. They're even better with an arrow at one end, charting the unequivocally most efficient path from Point A through Point B and beyond. Straight lines are easy to interpret. There's no lost energy dilly-dallying; it's self-evident where they're headed. The outcome is inevitable. Best of all, straight lines can be drawn from any point forward and also back in time—an after-the-fact exercise of connecting the dots to form a line.

When you're learning how to tell your life story in the context of a job search, straight lines are a helpful metaphor to organize the experiences you collect as you move through life. To an employer, your straight-line story is the reason why your path has inevitably led you to this job with this employer at this time—no matter how straight or curvy and meandering that line seemed as you were traveling it. Your straight line is a way to describe your professional journey as the confluence of your life and this job—the perfect match, planned or otherwise, seemingly driven by cosmic forces. It makes too much sense for it not to happen.

When you're good at successfully marketing yourself to prospective employers, you describe your experiences as if you've been executing your career development plan with foresight for years. Of course you probably didn't actually plan it that way, and you're not trying to convince the interviewer that you've spent your life on a mission that's been carved in stone since your crib days. But you can describe how your experiences form a straight line from relevant experiences in your life to the career you've chosen and the first job you seek.

Order in Chaos

Career experts have a fancy term they apply to this concept of a straight line only being evident in retrospect. They call it Chaos Theory. The central idea is that career paths generally aren't linear or predictable, and they often evolve in unexpected twists and turns. It's not an argument against planning. Rather, Chaos Theory calls for gaining comfort in ambiguity and developing the skill of adapting your plans as circumstances call for it. "It's kind of a looking backwards perspective," says the University of Georgia's Williams. "They don't even know how it's preparing them."

The University of Maryland's Bishop took it one step further. "For most people who are happy, it wasn't linear. If it had been linear, you would not be happy about it. You needed it not to be," he told me. "The difference is whether you can successfully engage in a way that's going to allow you to have the next opportunity. You may have a string of opportunities that bounce across different career fields and paths. But what you're invested in is your ability to make those leaps when you're ready—how to navigate across those different pathways."

You may not have thought of it this way, but in truth you've been building your career foundation every day. Some of it happens in the most obvious ways: your work in the classroom, or your time in a job or internship that's related to your career interests. That's important and good, but it's not at all the only way. Employers understand that most new college graduates don't have a ton of work experience. So they look for indicators—in all your activities—that you're the type of person who will adjust well to work life, and that being yourself will make you succeed. Some of those experiences build general traits such as leadership or ability to execute. They include "soft skills" like influencing, active listening, and working well with others. Some indicators simply show your ability to act on your passions and interests. Taken in total, they make a clear case that you have the skills and interests to succeed.

You've been accumulating these experiences in obvious and not so obvious ways.

I bet you didn't think your "R.A."—the student

resident assistant in your college dorm—was getting experience that future employers would value. But that experience matters to even the most prestigious companies who recruit college graduates to join their firms. All those petty arguments and concerns those advisors had to deal with were great training in dispute resolution, defusing out-of-control situations, and helping everyone get along and stay productive. "Former R.A.'s are great hires," Sean Treccia, director of global campus recruiting programs at Big Four accounting giant KPMG, told me.

You may think the athletes on campus were too busy lifting weights or practicing—in football, gymnastics, lacrosse, field hockey, or any sport—to be gaining useful career foundations. But those experiences are valued very highly by employers. Athletes generally have a zeal to win, they bounce back quickly from setbacks, and know what it's like to win and to lose. They have to excel at time management to balance sports and academics. Perhaps most importantly, they're coachable. They know how to take critical feedback and incorporate it into improved future performance. Those skills matter, too. Employers love athletes.

You might also think that being the president of an obscure club on campus is just a silly indulgence. But those experiences are valued by employers, too. They show an ability to pursue a passion, indulge an interest immersively, not to mention providing an opportunity to gain leadership and organizational experience. Moreover, they show a person with a drive to dive deeply into an activity, engage others, and grow—often moving out of ingrained comfort zones. Recruiters view this as a critical professional skill: the ability to embrace new situations, whether comfortable to you initially or not, and then reach a level of mastery through dedication and perseverance.

"I look at what you do during the school year, what you're involved with," Treccia said. "The kind of stuff I'm looking for is what are you doing to show you can balance school and work. I've interviewed the 4.0 student and I rejected them after the first interview because they had nothing else they had done."

The Explorer Within

In many ways, employers are a lot like the college admissions people you needed to impress to get into college in the first place. Yes, the basics like grades and test scores mattered then, and they set your baseline for admissibility. But it was more than that. Just as universities are looking for people who will contribute to campus life and not only succeed in the classrooms, employers are also looking for new hires who will enrich and enliven their culture and drive their work teams to peak performance.

College is for exploration of all sorts, both inside and outside the classroom, and employers are looking for new hires who have had successful campus careers overall by being active, curious, and engaged explorers. Don't overlook the important workplace traits that you've built—or some you never thought of as important—which are core to these experiences.

You probably have discovered key parts of your *ikigai* via these explorations, if you're paying attention. Some of those discoveries will come in direct ways, such as the student who decides on a career in medicine after spending time volunteering in a medical clinic. Other discoveries are more indirect, like the on-campus cafeteria job that unexpectedly shows how you have a knack for organizing and leading teams to get things done—even when they're not the most glamorous pursuits. The key is that the activities you participate in provide implicit and explicit clues to finding the most powerful inputs to your *ikigai*. Your job is to recognize them, to catalog them, and to be on the lookout for how to build on them by applying them to other experiences in the process of polishing your *ikigai*.

The element of *ikigai* that often comes last—and probably should—is how all your interest and skills lead to something that the world values enough to pay people like you to do it. You need a livelihood to reflect your passions and skills. You need to do it in a workplace—whether that workplace is in a traditional office, home office, or other setting. The entry ticket to the best jobs, of course, is work experience—ideally but not necessarily tied to the types of jobs you're targeting to start your work life after college. That's why it's so critically important to have internships and other work-related experiences during your college years—in addition to other activities. Internships are the most compelling evidence of many critical factors in the job search: they prove that your interest has been turned into action, and that you've proven to yourself that it actually interests you in practice, as learned via the intern experience. After all, if you had an internship you didn't enjoy, odds are you wouldn't be racing to do that job again full-time and set yourself off in that direction for your career path.

Internships used to be a differentiator, but in today's world they're assumed to be a part of your career preparation during your college years. New college graduates are expected to have had internships to be the best candidates for entry level jobs upon graduation. Today, it's only the candidates who have had multiple internships—and truly outstanding experiences during those internships and other activities—who stand out.

Any other type of on-the-job experience—whether part-time during the school year or 40 hours a week during a summer or a gap year—is a close second best to internships. Employers realize that many internships carry a social strata bias – they're often unpaid, or influenced by family or personal connections, so not an option for all students. Many students have no choice but to seek higher-paying jobs through their college years to pay for tuition and living expenses, or to contribute to supporting their families, and employers understand that. In fact, having this type of full-time work indicates several important traits that employers value, such as drive, work ethic, and a willingness to do what's needed to achieve the greater goal.

Any type of work experience—internships or other types of jobs—are important to employers for the most basic reasons: experience getting to work on time, being present and productive, managing your time well and being a good team player with colleagues of all ages. Employers would rather not gamble on your time in their office being your very first experience with those foundational aspects of work life.

Establishing Proof

There's also a third category of experiences—beyond activities and work or internship experience—that also matters to employers and can help you stand out. I call it 'proof'. Proof answers the question of why an employer should believe that your interest in a given career path is sincere. It's displayed by things like the people you speak with, what you research and what you read. For example, if you want to be a financial advisor, have you sought out family friends or other connections to be introduced to a financial advisor to learn more about what they do? Have you done any online research to understand what background is required to become a financial advisor? Do you visit any websites regularly to understand news and trends that are being talked about in the industry? These are easy to do, don't take a ton of time, and are things you should be doing anyway just to make an informed choice about whether a career direction is right for you. Moreover, they offer proof to an employer that you've taken initiative to not just speak about an interest, but to have taken actions to prove that interest is real. Follow the credo that an old boss of mine would often say: "Deeds, not words." What you do speaks louder than what you say, no matter how eloquently and persuasively you might say it.

The best way to gather these relevant experiences is to make career-related activities part of your routine early—even in high school, and certainly for the entirety of your college career, starting in your freshman year. Check in with your career center to learn about programs they have, particularly learning which companies routinely come to campus and host events for students. As a freshman or sophomore, these events are extremely valuable and low-pressure methods to learn about companies and the sorts of jobs they make available to interns and new graduates from your school. Plus you'll generally find free food and drinks, and you'll meet other students and learn from them why they're interested in that company. Other students are likely to have more, and different, information than the companies themselves will provide—often because they're in touch with alumni who currently work there.

Learn the rhythms of the calendar for organized recruitment on your campus. Much of the activity starts early in the fall term, with job fairs and other campus events hosted by employers. Interview season begins in earnest in the early Spring, even though the students who get hired won't start their jobs or internships until months later during the summer. Don't be left out because you didn't realize the companies you were interested in made their hiring decisions based on an already-completed interview season. Also, be mindful that your career center may have information about exceptional internship experiences during the school year—especially in larger cities where attractive employers are only a short walk or subway ride from your campus.

When you plan to attend on-campus events, don't apply too much of a filter to which companies seem to be a fit for you. Just show up, listen and think about the possibilities. Is this something I could see myself doing? Do I have things in common with graduates of my school who chose to work there? Would working at this place be the absolute worst match for me on every level? All of those questions will yield valid impressions, but keep an open mind and learn more about the range of options than you knew going in. And who knows—you might be captivated by an industry, role, or locale that you had never considered before.

CHAPTER 3 EXERCISE

☐ Visit your campus career center website and look for
upcoming events, particularly those that are hosted
by companies who hire from your school and have
an open house or presentation scheduled. Make a
list of the events you want to attend, and don't want
to attend, and write a list of all your reasons why
for each. You'll start to learn things about yourself
that you maybe didn't know. It's also a good idea
to then go ahead and attend a few events that were
on your 'don't go' list just as a check to see if your
instincts were correct. It never hurts to keep an open
mind and gauge your reactions to lots of different
experiences.

CHAPTER 4

POWER OF INTERNSHIPS

If you're still in college, get an internship. Even after you've graduated, get an internship. In fact, get at least two to three internships—or more. There's no getting around it: internships are far and away the number-one type of experience that will impress recruiters and propel your full-time work career. Other experiences count too, both inside and outside the classroom, and more types of experiences are now valued by employers as they look for new blood to join their organizations. But working as an intern—ideally as a full-time role for about 10-12 weeks during a summer or other time off from school—is the keystone to a well-rounded post-college resume

A lot of that, selfishly for you, is good for your career exploration and data gathering. Having an internship is your own test drive of what it's really like to work in a given industry, company, or role. You'll see the truth every day of what it's really like. What's it really like to be a doctor, a researcher, or a marketer? What's it really like to work in fashion, in retail, or in a hotel or a hospital? You might fall in love with it. You might think it's awful and you couldn't stand to ever do it again for even a day, let alone full-time as a career path. Trust your instincts about those experiences, because they all matter and are probably spot on for you. And don't fret if you've had an internship in an industry you thought you'd love but have since learned is not for you. That's not a wasted summer. Quite the contrary, you've learned a valuable lesson and new potential employers will be glad you've had the experience, too.

Companies evaluating you as a candidate are looking for a few things in your internship and other work history. The most basic is having experience going to work every day instead of school, getting to interact with people in that professional setting who may be quite older than you but performing similar tasks, and completing assignments in a work setting.

Here's a news flash: work isn't school. Have you had to get up in the morning, get to the office (even virtually) on time, stay there all day, act professionally, and get things done? That sounds simplistic, but those experiences are the basic building blocks to success in a workplace setting—even as some of that is finding new forms in remote work. There are similarities to school, but it's a very different routine. Beyond those basics, companies want to learn about the content of your experiences in an internship because they're trying to project how you'll perform in their environment. If you loved your internship and want to find full-time work in the same industry, then potential employers will see your internship as proof of your specific interest in them. That counts! Employers want to be wanted, too. Nobody wants to hire the "I don't care, I just want a job" candidate.

Employers used to think of internships as a quasi-public service—a way for companies to give back to their communities by offering students the experience of being able to observe and do very low-level tasks in an office environment. They typically had very low pay, or no pay at all, yet offered more experience in memorizing coffee orders than providing meaningful value to companies. Even many large companies typically hired low numbers of interns. But that has all changed. Internships are now offered at large and small companies, with gofer tasks not in the job description, creating valuable experiences to interns and a reliable pipeline of talent for full-time roles when those students graduate.

The Internship Machine

For many employers, internships are part of a large-scale, highly coordinated and data-driven strategy to bring new talent into their companies. The largest of these employers hire thousands of interns and thousands more new college grads every single year. Some have dozens of employees whose sole role at the company is managing the recruiting and work experiences of interns. Here are the companies that planned to do the most hiring in 2020 according to CollegeGrad.com's annual survey:

INTERN HIRES FOR 2020

Employer Name	Planned 2020 Hires
EY	4,000
Deloitte	3,800
KPMG	3,800
New York Life Insurance Co.	3,500
PwC	3,100
Google	2,200
Southwestern Advantage	2,015
Enterprise Rent-A-Car	2,000
Northwestern Mutual Life Insurance	2,000
Intel	1,600

Source: Others with 1,000 or more planned intern hires were Amazon.com, Lockheed Martin, General Electric, Dell, Quicken Loans, Microsoft, and Raytheon.

A lot of the same names are on this list of companies doing the most hiring of new college graduates. In most cases, the hires on this list are populated mostly from interns during the prior year.

ENTRY-LEVEL HIRES FOR 2020

Employer Name	Planned 2020 Hires
Enterprise Rent-A-Car	8,500
Deloitte	5,600
EY	5,000
Hertz	5,000
The Progressive Corp	4,200
KPMG	4,100
PwC	3,900
Revature	3,000
Federal Bureau of Investigation	2,900
Avis Budget Group	2,500

Others with 1,000 or more planned entry-level hires were Bank of America, U.S. Customs and Border Protection, Google, Epic, Raytheon, Amazon.com, Intel, MGM Resorts International, National Security Agency, PNC Financial Services Group, Chevron, Sodexo, Southwest Airlines, Walmart Stores, Cigna, Lockheed Martin, Microsoft, Vanguard, Finish Line, C.H. Robinson Worldwide, Dell, Fastenal, Mutual of Omaha Insurance Co., R1 RCM, Staples, Total Quality Logistics, U.S. Air Force, U.S. Department of Labor, and U.S. Department of State.

That's a lot of interns and new hires! Surely, those numbers are somewhat depressed for actual 2020 hiring because of the coronavirus pandemic. But don't expect those numbers to dwindle forever. Historically, the totals are fairly consistent year to year. For these large-scale companies, the intern and entry-level hiring pipeline is the shark that must keep swimming to keep up its oxygen flow. Interns become full-time hires, and entry-level hires soon move up to fill the mid-level managerial ranks. In good times, the new hire programs breed healthy new talent that these companies rely upon to identify and nurture their future leaders. Even with the coronavirus interruption, you can bet that these same companies will seek to replenish their stock as quickly as possible. It's their lifeblood. These large companies with armies of interns and new grad hires simply can't afford to have a large gap in their succession planning.

For these companies, the decision to hire in such high volume reflects a highly considered business decision based on cold, hard data. Michael van Grinsven, who ran the internship program at financial services giant Northwestern Mutual for 35 years, told me the company's decision to hire 2,000 interns annually was based on one of its core competencies: analyses run by the company's own actuarial data experts. The data told them that a college intern who converted to a full-time hire was worth three times the value of someone who joined the company via a mid-career shift—even when hired just a few years after new hires who joined straight out of college. Interns who converted to full-time roles had a head start with great advantages. Not only did they learn the company, but they got valuable experience directly with clients very early in their careers, even as interns. "At a lot of internships, you're behind the scenes, doing stuff for the (financial) advisor. Our program allowed them to work side by side with the advisor and at some points be client-facing on their own," van Grinsven explained. "The ability to ask good questions, handle objections, clarify things: they learned how to navigate through all that. They could model that and replicate that in the future because they'd seen it up close."

At the companies doing the highest volume hiring for interns and new grad hires, the recruiting engine is a high-octane machine. At KPMG, for example, which is the smallest of the Big Four accounting firms yet still has more than 200,000 employees globally, a staff of 160 people is required to recruit their interns and entry-level hires for North America alone. Teams like that are in effect a fully functioning small business within a large enterprise, with more people than the entire staff at some of the well-funded startups I've worked for. A single college recruiter might spend 50 days a year on-campus at a large university with a top accounting program, and hire 100 or more students from a single school. The goal of the internship from KPMG's perspective is clear: hire them full-time. According to KPMG's Treccia, the internal goal is to convert 92% of interns to full-time employees. That leaves far fewer spots available for graduating seniors who were not part of the intern program. Only 10-15% of new hires are seniors who didn't get their start as a KPMG intern.

The lesson to college students is clear. If you wait until your senior year to try to join a company like KPMG, the odds are stacked against you because so many of their spots are already filled by those who had internships just prior to their senior year. Not much is left for the seniors meeting KPMG for the first time. "Full-time recruiting is to fill in the gaps," Treccia says. "You want to get as many as you can through the internship." That's why advance planning from the student's perspective is paramount. This voyage starts early. The numbers work in your favor if you board the train as an intern rather than waiting to squeeze in as a senior when most of the seats are already filled.

The Intern's Path

To keep those intern-to-full-time conversion statistics strong, companies put a lot of effort into ensuring a good internship experience. SAS, a major analytics software provider based in North Carolina that employs thousands of people worldwide, hires about 400 interns and new entry-level hires each year, according to Kayla Woitkowski, who runs university outreach and recruiting for the company. Every proposed internship across the company must pass through what they call an 'allocation process' to define, justify, and plan each intern's experience to assure that it's meaningful for the intern as well as valuable to SAS. If the plan isn't good enough, that department gets no interns. Plus, managers who get interns receive special training from Woitkowski's team to get tips on how to manage interns during their 10-week program. At a large program like that, there's no alternative. There are simply too many interns in too many locations to leave to chance that the company gets its return on investment. SAS wants to provide a robust internship experience that attracts the best talent to come back full-time. But the company also wants to assure that they've had enough opportunity to see the intern in action to know which ones deserve the offer to return.

During the program, interns and their managers at SAS do frequent check-ins with Woitkowski's team to assure the experience is working well, or making any program adjustments as necessary on a per-intern basis—even with virtual experiences during the pandemic. And the summer concludes with a survey to assess each intern's experience from all sides. Why is all that necessary? "Our intern program is our pipeline for future talent for our organization," Woitkowski explains. "It's an essential element of our workforce planning."

The advantage of initially joining a company as an intern isn't just a fact of life at SAS, the Big Four accounting firms, or any of the largest companies. It's increasingly the norm as more firms realize the cost efficiencies of hiring interns whom they can convert to full-time roles. "There is a lot more emphasis on internship recruiting right now," the University of Georgia's Williams said. "Employers are using conversion rates—how successful they are at turning interns into full-time hires, and that's driving a greater effort on internships." Those companies can attract top talent, give them a great experience, bolster their employment brands and get a 10-week internship audition prior to making a job offer. That makes a lot more sense to companies than taking the greater risk of hiring students they only get to meet for a few hours in interviews prior to having them join the company.

Williams told me about a large pharmaceutical company that used to reliably interview and hire six to ten seniors from his campus every year to take on fairly lucrative sales jobs. "Now if you're a senior and looking to get hired at that company, you're probably not going to get a job because they're having so much success converting their interns to full-time," Williams said. "For those interns, the positive thing is they come back to school and they have job offers. They're going to be entry-level pharmaceutical sales reps. I've seen a bigger push in that direction."

From the candidate perspective, these large-scale internship and entry-level programs are terrific launching pads whether or not you see a long-term career path in one of those companies. Surely, the direct path is a valid one: join a company as an intern, sign on for an entry-level job, work your way up through middle management and then ascend to an executive role in that firm. That's a viable straight-line career path, with clear milestones and opportunities for advancement. Especially at those large companies, advancement into management can be quite lucrative. But these programs are also well known as de facto training programs for other companies. For example, you may not have grown up with stars in your eyes, dreaming about a career at Enterprise Rent-A-Car. But other companies love hiring 'graduates' of Enterprise's program because of the terrific training that's available there—probably more experience in managing people, dealing with customers, and problem resolution than one could get at many other jobs with that level of experience. And many new hires in the Enterprise program, of course, move up swiftly in the company's management ranks when they choose to stay on.

"Every other company loves Enterprise," I was told by D.J. Washington, a senior executive at The Athlete Network, which helps companies and college athletes find each other for career opportunities. "What typically happens is they mold them, and a lot of other companies benefit from it. They love the training."

Of course, equally if not superior internship experiences are available at smaller companies without the large-volume programs like Enterprise, SAP, or any of the others hiring hundreds to thousands of interns and entry-level graduates every year. Even when you're the only intern, or the first intern the company has ever had, there are valuable experiences to be had via internships. The greatest difference in a smaller or new program is the work you as the intern will need to do during the ten or so weeks you're on the job. That time goes fast, and you need to be thinking ahead to how you'll be describing the most valuable elements of your internship on your resume—and to potential future employers—during your next hiring cycle (either your next internship or your first full-time job upon graduation). As you plan for your internship, think ahead to the interviews you'll have later—and the bullet points you'll be able to add to your resume to describe the experience—and assure that you have great things to talk about from your time as an intern.

Internships and your *Ikigai*

Your intern experience is a great teacher. It tells you what you didn't know about yourself: what you like, what rubs you the wrong way, what excites you and makes you wish for more, and what you should run away from. Trust your instincts. There's a lot to absorb, and a lot to experience to help you polish your *ikigai* and confirm or disprove things you thought about yourself and your interests. Is this really the industry you thought you'd enjoy, or the function you thought would be interesting, or the type of company that lights your fire? Your internship—so long as your observational powers are in high gear—will let you know.

My son Graydon's experience in two of his internships were a stark contrast, which helped him immensely as he thought about what he wanted to do after college. On paper, two of his internships were identically strong—one at Giorgio Armani, and the other at Cartier. But to Graydon, they could not have been more different. Armani, he thought, had a dispiriting 'mean girls' culture—one that took advantage of interns and offered very little of substance in the work he was asked to do. Thankfully, he had some very limited exposure to a few of Armani's private selling events, which he helped execute, and which formed the takeaway narrative for the experience that he could describe in future interviews. But mostly, it helped him to recognize signs of a culture he wanted to avoid in the future. Cartier, though, had a fantastic culture: professional and courteous in every way. While Graydon surmised quickly that his passions didn't match with his functional role in Cartier's retail operations group, his managers recognized it and helped make introductions for a small amount of his summer to be spent with the company's marketing team. That, as it turned out, would be his chosen functional path into Gucci as his first full-time job after college.

In sum, Graydon's internship experiences taught him what he liked and what he wanted to avoid. The marquee names on his resume were certainly powerful, but the insights he gained about how to steer his career were invaluable.

Another lesson from those experiences: stick to it. Graydon was rejected at first for both the Armani and Cartier internships, as well as his first one at Marc Jacobs. They said no. But Graydon stayed in touch with his contacts at each company and kept inquiring about other possibilities, and in each case a new internship opportunity indeed surfaced. That's the power of perseverance.

Also, not every employer plans in advance for its summer needs, so there are still internships looking for students as late as June and even July—fewer, to be sure, but still enough to be worth your time to keep tabs. One trend that popped up in Summer 2020 was the "mini internship"—small projects that students could complete on their own in as little as one week. Mini internships are likely to reflect immediate needs for companies who wish they had an intern, but don't.

If your internship was cancelled, you'd be well served to reach out to the person who would have been your boss, and ask if there are any projects you could do as a mini internship. There are also clearinghouses for mini internship work, such as Parker Dewey, where you can learn about mini internship opportunities such as cleaning up data or performing a social media competitive review.

Assuring your Internship's Value

For any internship, whether at one of the large companies with established internship programs, or an ad hoc internship at a smaller company, it's your job as the intern to assure that you get the most out of the experience. It's actually very hard work for managers to craft meaningful projects on their own. Most of the time, they don't have to think in a ten-week chunk of time with a new worker, so crafting a project that's useful to both the company and the intern takes some creativity and forethought. That's where your contribution comes in, and your work should begin before you even start the internship. Correspond with your manager-to-be prior to the internship and ask what specific project or projects you'll get the chance to pursue. The response will be a clue as to how much effort has already been put into figuring that out. If the answer is vague, you know you'll have your work cut out for you once you arrive on the job. In a typical ten-week internship, you'll want to be sure you have identified and gained traction on a meaningful project no later than two to three weeks into your internship. That still leaves several weeks to perform the project and present your results to managers at the company. The best way to identify a project is to ask for time with your new colleagues on the job, find out what they wish they could work on but can't because of other priorities, or just ask them what they're working on and find a way to contribute that interests you.

My own experience as an intern may be a useful guide. Between my first and second years of business school, I interned in the financial planning department at the Los Angeles Times newspaper. Early in my summer internship, I overheard a conversation about the paper's special advertising sections, which were one-time or once-a-year sections in the paper to commemorate major events like a sports team's championship or the annual Rose Bowl parade. The finance folks groused that these advertising sections weren't the revenue booster that those in the advertising sales group said they were. Instead, my finance colleagues argued, there was probably a significant amount of "switch business," meaning that regular advertisers simply switched their planned advertising from the regular sections of the newspaper to the special section. If true, it meant that these sections provided scant true incremental revenue, and in fact were a drain on profitability because of added cost to produce. I found this interesting and theorized that the argument could be settled with a small project, which I proposed. My project—which involved a fair amount of manual effort tracking data in the newspaper's advertising invoice systems—studied the patterns of ad purchases in the weeks before and after the six largest special sections of the prior year. I found that the finance folks were correct, and I got to present those findings to the heads of the newspaper's financial planning and advertising teams. As a result, the paper cut back its publication of special sections, so my work had an impact. That was a fantastic talking point to take with me from that summer experience, and probably the key to getting a full-time job offer at The Times upon graduating from business school. You'll want to be equally proactive, or more so, in assuring the best experience at your internship. By being proactive, and listening for work that should be done but the full-time team doesn't have time to do, you can seek to add work to your internship that will make your time more valuable to you and the company. A classic win-win.

When Internships Aren't Available

You may be surprised to learn that the National Association of College and Employers (NACE)—the association whose membership includes college career center people and employers who hire new college graduates—recommends that accepted-but-cancelled internships should still be listed on your LinkedIn profile and resume. "XYZ Company—Internship offer accepted. Rescinded due to Covid-19—Summer 2020," is how they say to do it. Recruiters in a NACE survey said adding the lost internship shows many positives. Among them: you had the initiative to get the internship in the first place, you had the learning experience of job loss, and it explains why you didn't have an internship for that period. But recruiters are quick to add: you should do everything you can to add experiences for the time you had planned to be at your internship. Sedentarily sitting at home won't look good on your resume. Video game proficiency and Netflix aren't transferable skills for most jobs!

Here are five other things you can do to be productive with your time if internships aren't an option, but you'd like to acquire meaningful experiences anyway:

- **Volunteer:** If you have the means to work for free, then volunteering is a great way to offer your skills to for-profit and non-profit entities. Be creative in assessing how you can add value. The more it relates to a possible career path, the better. Help out a small business by offering to build out its social profiles and social posts, or getting its receipts in order to make the bookkeeper's job easier (and thereby cheaper for the business you assist). Find a local charitable organization that needs extra hands. Volunteer opportunities, if you have the luxury to pursue them, are terrific opportunities to showcase your skills while you help others.

- **Network:** Create or update your LinkedIn profile, and build connections with friends, ex co-workers, and family members—and those they know—who already work in industries that interest you.

- **Take online classes:** Self-paced learning opportunities are everywhere on the Internet, and there are myriad skills you should probably have but haven't yet developed. Some of the best to consider are those skills that probably aren't taught as part of your college curriculum. Take a class on advanced techniques for Excel or Powerpoint. Learn a new program like business analytics, or acquire a good working knowledge of an emerging technology like data science or artificial intelligence. Improve your public speaking or presentation skills. In short, get better. Some colleges provide free access to LinkedIn Learning, which has a wide variety of terrific online courses.

- **Enhance your portfolio:** Almost every job description you'll read says the position requires outstanding written and oral communications skills, yet most people could stand to improve substantially in those skills. As a former newspaper reporter, I know from personal experience that the best way to be a better writer is to write.

"Take solace in the fact that you were already vetted by an employer as a desirable candidate," advises the University of Maryland's Bishop. "Although they may not be able to bring you on board as planned, they very likely want to remain connected. You represent the 'front of the line' when they are able to recommence hiring."

CHAPTER 4 EXERCISES

☐ Identify companies doing the most on-campus internship hiring at your school, and develop a short list of those that interest you.

☐ Make a list of skills you want to improve on, which will be your go-to if you find yourself with time between jobs and can stay occupied with productive online learning.

CHAPTER 5

ELEVATOR PITCH

Your elevator pitch is the story you tell that draws your straight line directly to a job that matches your *ikigai*—two concepts described earlier in this book. Remember, you're the product. So your elevator pitch is what's written in your very own advertising copy—about you! It's the clearest distillation of how you'll market yourself to future employers. It's concise, punchy, interesting and differentiating. It's called an elevator pitch because it can be delivered quickly, as in the time it takes to take a typical ride in an elevator: not much time at all. Most important, it's a story that's compelling for its sense of inevitability. You want company recruiters to think, "Of course your path leads you to this career, and this job, at this company. We'd be so lucky to have you." Match made.

An ideal elevator pitch tells how your experiences—in school, in your work, and your personal passions—point an arrow directly to your chosen career path. It provides proof that your interest in a particular career is genuine and makes sense. Sometimes, the path is straightforward. For example, it's easy for a pre-med student to develop an elevator pitch to interview for a research internship at a hospital after having completed several science classes and volunteering at another hospital. In other cases, it requires a bit more imagination to come up with a winning pitch. For example, the elevator pitch for a graduating senior wanting to enter management consulting might include academic performance, leadership in school-related projects, and working summers in the family business to learn about how a business works from the inside.

Most recruiters' number-one pet peeve is speaking with candidates who clearly haven't thought through why they're even sitting for the interview. They can't tell their story—a clear statement of who they are and why it makes sense for them to be sitting down to talk about their match to that company in particular.

"Work where it makes you happy," advises KPMG's Treccia. "When you ask a student, 'Why did you major in x?' and you hear 'Oh, my parents told me it was good,' or 'My professor told me it's good,' that's fine when you're 16, but when you're 20 and you're starting to look for a job, what do you want to do?".

How do you determine what to emphasize in an elevator pitch? The answer is quite personal and unique to you, based on your demonstrated passions and interests. 'Demonstrated' is the key, because it's not just about what you want to do, but what you've done already in your life that points your straight line toward what you want to do. You can demonstrate that direction by work you've done, classes you've taken, life experiences you've had, and even the periodicals you read to stay abreast of news in your chosen field. How you demonstrate your interest brings credibility to why you're there delivering your elevator pitch, and when executed well it will help you stand out.

Competencies

You'll also want to remember the career competencies described earlier in this book as you prepare your elevator pitch. Your goal in any pitch is to display your above-average skills in at least three of those eight competencies as they apply to you. Which are the ones that you know you seem to be better at than a lot of people you know—your special traits? Let's review the competencies again, and what sorts of experiences speak to them:

- **Professionalism:** Do you have experience in a work setting and know how to conduct yourself there, including how to dress, when to show up, and how you find productive things to do? Are you a self-starter who has found high-value things to do without having had to be asked to do them?

- **Leadership:** In what ways have you led others, either as a formal leader (e.g. team captain, club president) or in other ways that you contribute in group settings to elevate your team's performance?

- **Communication:** Are you a capable speaker and writer? This comes through loud and clear in interviews based on the succinctness and thoughtfulness of your answers. It's also revealed in how you write your resume, cover letters, and even email correspondence to set up an interview.

- **Career Management:** Do you have a realistic understanding of what it will take to build your career beyond the entry level? Can you articulate a sensible plan and reasonable timeline of how you expect to progress in your career?

- **Problem Solving:** Can you demonstrate how you have faced problems—personal, academic, or professional—and that you took actions to resolve them using a combination of fact-finding, analysis, and interpersonal skills?

- **Intercultural Fluency:** Are you able to empathetically interact and team with people from other cultures, and have you sought to involve yourself in situations with people unlike yourself? Do you have experience venturing outside your comfort zone?

- **Teamwork:** Are you a good team member—a leader and supporter of others—whether in formal leadership roles or as an engaged contributor?

- **Digital Technology:** Are you facile with modern technologies including knowledge of basic business software (e.g. word processing, spreadsheet, presentation) and capable of quickly learning how to use new software?

The best personal statements are those that underscore very strong and above-average capabilities and aptitude on your three chosen competencies—with real-world examples to tell your story. Think hard and you'll find your best competencies and how to describe them. "Regardless of what major they secured, it doesn't matter if it's Philosophy or Electrical Engineering—they have developed some of those career competencies through their academic curriculum," says Williams of the University of Georgia. "It's just a matter of articulating them, and sometimes that's a challenge for them."

The straight lines you describe in your elevator pitch will become your stock answer to the "Tell me about yourself" question that very commonly kicks off many interviews. It's your opportunity to set a tone for the conversation, and to distinguish yourself as a compelling, differentiated product. As with a presidential candidate on the campaign trail, the personal statement is your stump speech. It's got common core elements that with practice you can roll out anytime. It's tailored on the edges for specific audiences, but its basics are identical and paint a clear and compelling picture of who you are, and what makes you interesting and distinctly valuable.

Here's a fictional example of a skeleton elevator pitch based on a straight line. We'll make up a new friend; we'll call him Paul. Let's say Paul wants to start a career in sales. Paul has had a few activities, but not many: he was president of a photography club in college, was a theater major but took a few courses in marketing and psychology, and had a summer job as an office worker at a public relations agency. His mother was a pharmaceutical salesperson before going to medical school. Where's the straight line? Well, the club experience was a leadership role and our buddy Paul did a great job of growing its membership. In a Film class, he studied Glengarry Glen Ross, a classic movie about a cutthroat, high-pressure sales organization. His marketing class covered market segmentation, and his psychology class included studies on motivation and productivity. Paul's mom liked to tell stories about how she learned about hospital work during her days in sales. That might sound like a hodgepodge, but there's' a lot there to draw a straight line through. Here's what Paul's stump speech might sound like when a job interview starts with, "Tell me about yourself, Paul."

"Well, I grew up hearing about the right way to do sales from my mother, who did pharmaceutical sales before she went to medical school. And I learned the wrong way to do it in a Film class in college where we studied the movie Glengarry Glen Ross. I got my own taste of the excitement of closing in my time as a club president in college, drawing on some lessons from a marketing class I took, and growing membership in the club. Now I want to take those skills into a professional selling environment. I've learned a lot about selling by listening to the buyer's perspective—something that draws on what I learned in my psychology classes—and I'm excited to put that into practice starting my career."

Not a bad start on the bones of a 'straight line' elevator pitch! It's genuine and personal. It hits on a few important career competencies: professionalism from getting kitchen table training from his mother about selling, leadership from his time as a club president, and career management from his understanding of what it takes to move up in the company. Our friend Paul has a lot to work with to create a very compelling elevator pitch.

Tailoring the Pitch

Now, how do we tailor the stump speech for a particular opportunity? That involves a little preparation and research—most commonly from a job description you can study, or basic online research you can do on the company's website before an interview. For example, you can find out whether there's a training program at the company you're interviewing with, or what other full-time roles exist that represent a solid promotion path upward at the company. So Paul might add this to his elevator pitch:

"I'm really excited to be speaking with you today because I know your company has an excellent training program. I've read that people who do well in that program have opportunities for international roles, which I'm very interested in doing at some point in my career."

An impressive start! A little bit of customized preparation goes a long way in putting the finishing touches on your pitch for a particular meeting. That's what an elevator pitch is all about. It's easy to do, the preparation research doesn't need to take much time at all, and it's hugely differentiating for you as a candidate. Here's why: hardly anyone does it. And that makes it so easy for you to stand out by doing it right.

Let's dive in a little further to show how to craft a truly outstanding pitch. Think broadly about it. Be sure to consider all your experiences—inside the classroom, in activities and professional settings. You're the product, so to succeed in selling your product, you need to tailor your pitch to the needs of the 'buyer'—in this case the interviewer or recruiter representing an employer. Think about the distinctive traits and experiences that make you special as it relates to the company's needs and the position you're speaking about. Make it interesting and different. Show examples of going outside of your comfort zone.

"If they're from Chicago and they're an accounting major in the business school, and you see every group they're in has people from their high school and they're all accounting majors, and every intramural they play on is with the same group of kids, that's a little concerning," KPMG's Treccia told me. "What we're looking for is if you've put yourself out there and challenged yourself, if you've been willing to put yourself in uncomfortable situations, even if you've failed and learned from it."

Failure is interesting and genuine, overcoming failure shows perseverance, and being comfortable talking about it shows humility—so those are great interview anecdotes. "The students who give examples of everything they've done being a super success, I worry about that," Treccia said. "They're going to fail. We all fail. I look for ones who can tell me what they learned when it didn't work out. How did you take the feedback and how did you learn from it? That means a lot more than someone who has never made a mistake."

One thing you should have noticed about all those elevator pitch statements: there was never a 'we' to describe accomplishments (or failures), but always statements that start with 'I.' Interviewers expect you to have a proper balance of describing yourself positively but without coming off as pompous. You need to show you're a great teammate and display humility, but they're still there to consider hiring you, not everyone else you worked with. They want to know what you did, so get comfortable with the idea of using 'I' way more than 'we.'

"You're taught to share the credit, but when you're interviewing, I want to know what you did," Treccia shared. "I want to know how you interacted with the team, but I also want to know what your role was. Some students talk about 'We did this,' 'We did that.' That's great because we don't want them being arrogant, but sometimes we have to dig in and say "Ok, what did you specifically do in that team?" Don't make your interviewer work that hard. Mention the team but concentrate on you.

CHAPTER 5 EXERCISE

☐ Craft your own elevator pitch by thinking about your experiences, and how you have exhibited at least three of the eight competencies described in this chapter. Write it down, edit it, then edit again. It will take some work to get it right. Practice in front of a mirror, record it on Zoom and critique it yourself, and then try it on a friend or counselor.

CHAPTER 6

YOUR RESUME

Curriculum vitae, the fancy Latin term for a resume, translates to 'the course of one's life.' That's a pretty broad term, as the course of your life is an expansive set of rich and interwoven experiences, influences, learnings, and accomplishments. Taken literally, a curriculum vitae—CV, for short—would be a detailed compilation of oodles of detail. Put another way, a true curriculum vitae would be so torturously long, self-indulgent, and overbearing that virtually no one would read it—maybe not even the person it's about, or even their parents. Sounds like no one would even bother to write one, right?

Yet most resumes are written as if the true meaning of curriculum vitae, in all its verbose glory, were still the implied objective. They're commonly just laundry lists of disconnected factoids rather than being what they should be, which is a strategically driven and purposeful document with a focus on details from your background that are relevant to a specific objective—getting the type of job for which you're applying at the moment.

Most people, when sitting down to compose their own resume, start off in the wrong place. They think in isolation about how to describe the jobs they've had in the past, which sounds reasonable enough, except that what they spent the bulk of their time doing in a given job is mostly beside the point. What matters far more are the types of experiences and achievements you had in each of those roles that are most important and meaningful relative to your particular career objectives at any given time.

I call this phenomenon the "90/10 Fallacy," meaning that most people in writing a resume try to summarize how they spent 90% of their time in a particular experience rather than the 10% that's most important to getting their next job. The 90% thinkers believe that capturing what they did most of the time in a given role is the best way to describe it. But therein lies the fallacy. Your resume is not a collection of job descriptions from your prior work. Rather, it's a summary of the most important experiences you gained, and accomplishments you achieved in those jobs that are relevant to the type of role you're targeting for your next job. Surely, how you spent the bulk of your time may be relevant. But it's far better to think about what you did that tells a new employer how qualified you are for the next job, rather than how much time you spent doing it.

Remember our fictional friend Paul? Let's engage him again and say he spent a summer as an intern in the sales department of an Internet software startup. For his most time-consuming project, he did the important but rather tedious work of online research and phone-calling to confirm sales prospects' titles in the company's contacts database. That's not very flashy stuff, and maybe shouldn't even make the cut to be on Paul's resume. But Paul also spent a week analyzing sales data and speaking to salespeople about a new feature the company had introduced that summer, and got to present his findings and recommendations to the team's sales managers. That's a terrific internship experience, and should certainly be what Paul emphasizes most in his resume, even though it didn't take up a large percentage of his overall internship time.

Bad resumes, even when well written, are just a recitation of the activities that have consumed your time, rather than a highlight reel of the spare set of experiences that illustrate why you're such a great fit for a specific type of job. Make sure you don't write a bad resume. Be dynamic and celebrate the accomplishments that matter most.

Using Bullet Points

Those most important elements of your prior job, based on their relevance to the type of job you're seeking, are contained in bullet points under each company you list on your resume. Ideally, they're two to three bullet points that highlight the most relevant elements of that experience from a future employer's perspective. Bullet points give punch to your resume. They describe your contributions in a way that makes employers wish you were on their team.

Strong bullet points start with powerful active verbs like "Drove," "Initiated," or "Built," rather than passive or low-impact, humdrum words such as "Responsible for," "Prepared," or "Attended." Ideally, bullet points have what resume experts call PAR statements, which stands for Problem, Action, Result. In other words, a PAR statement describes how you took action to fix a problem, resulting in a measurable, favorable result. A resume expert once told me the best PAR statement he had ever read went something like this: "Inherited the most robbed bank in Los Angeles County, then conceived and implemented new safety procedures leading to 50% reduction in thefts within three months." Talk about a memorable statement that makes you want to buy that product, or in this case hire that bank manager!

Good bullet points make an interviewer want to meet you to ask more about the story behind what you've written. Wouldn't you want to talk to that bank manager to learn more about those bank robberies?

As an entry-level candidate, you'll want to limit yourself to two or at most three bullet points per role. As a general rule, you want to have the most bullet points for the jobs that have the most pre-professional relevance, and have fewer or even no bullet points for jobs that most people—yourself included—would agree don't relate much to your professional abilities. You never want to puff up a job to make it sound like more than it really was. For example, if you spent a summer answering phones in a law office, you don't have to agonize over how to make that sound like you were clerking for a Supreme Court justice. Simply note the experience, perhaps with one bullet point at most. Save space for multiple bullet points where it really matters: jobs that exhibit your professional skills and workplace competencies the best.

Here are some example active verbs that could be associated with each of the professional competencies mentioned earlier in this book. Of course, there are many more active verbs to match the activities you'll highlight, but these will be useful as thought starters.

- **Professionalism:** Managed, executed, headed, achieved, coached

- **Leadership:** Led, drove, initiated, organized, oversaw, established

- **Communication:** Wrote, crafted, presented, convinced, documented

- **Career Management:** Planned, advanced, promoted

- **Problem Solving:** Solved, fixed, conceived, diagnosed, analyzed

- **Intercultural Fluency:** Engaged, joined, translated

- **Teamwork:** Coordinated, contributed, helped, influenced

- **Digital Technology:** Built, programmed, devised

Resume Formats

Strong, active verbs are part of any resume, but where they go depends on what style of resume you create. You need to decide what kind of resume is most appropriate for you.

You may be tempted to use one of the newer, more creative resume formats created by talented visual designers who I'm sure view the standard resume formats as way too staid, boring, and yesterday. Trouble is, the first and sometimes only one who reviews your resume may not be a person, but instead a computer trained to scan your resume for key terms only. All the visually arresting elements of these high-concept resume formats will probably leave you handcuffed in the eyes of the computer. It certainly won't see those parts of your resume, and worse still, the computer may misinterpret the bits and bytes it sees in the graphics. While it's true that not all companies use a form of computerized resume screening, using graphics and overly cutesy formatting really is not worth the risk. My advice: show your creativity in other ways, and stick to the basics when preparing your resume.

There are really only two main families of choices for a standard resume—a chronological resume or a functional resume. Each has all the same basic core elements, such as what your key skills are and where you've worked. The difference between them is what is emphasized—experience or skills. A chronological resume puts the jobs you've had front and center, while a functional resume cedes center stage to your skills. The real key to choosing which type is best for you is how much professional work experience you've had, and how relevant that work experience is to the work you're trying to get. If you haven't had much work experience, or the jobs you've had aren't very relevant to the jobs you're trying to get, then a functional resume might be the best choice for you. But if you've had good work experience and can write strong bullet points describing your work there, then a chronological resume is best.

All things equal, you'd rather have a chronological resume than a functional one. That's what recruiters and hiring managers would rather see. But if a functional resume is best for you, then go with that. A quick Google search will yield countless examples of chronological and functional resumes that match your career interests.

Whichever style of resume you choose, be sure to keep these elements in mind:

- **Restrict your resume to one page only.** More than one page is a turnoff, given that college students and recent grads generally haven't yet achieved a significant professional pedigree. Recruiters will think you're being pretentious by going over one page. Save your two-page or longer resume for when you're in your 30s and later.

- **Don't crowd your layout.** Make it easy to read by using no less than one-inch or 1.5-inch margins, and 10- or 12-point standard fonts. Save your resume in pdf format so you are certain that all your hard work on formatting is viewable exactly as you've created it—for the real-live humans who see it after those computers have completed their initial screening.

- **Remember the journalist's credo: every writer needs an editor.** Show your resume to others to assure that it's easy to understand and contains no typos. You'll need to write and revise your resume multiple times anyway, in order to get a resume in the exact shape you want it. Engaging others in the process is helpful—and confidence-boosting, too.

- **Skim your resume to assure you've chosen the best active verbs**, and don't re-use them if you can avoid it. Eliminating repeated words in any type of writing is always a good practice.

Objective or Summary

Regardless of whether you've chosen a chronological or functional resume, it's always a good idea to put an Objective or Summary statement right under your contact information at the top of the page. Think of it as the resume equivalent of your elevator pitch. It stresses your overall positioning and why you're such a great fit for the type of job you're seeking. The difference between an Objective and a Summary is based on your candid self-appraisal of how much experience you already have for the job you want. A Summary distills the things you've already done that relate directly to the type of job you're seeking. It shows your more direct path: If you majored in accounting, worked summers in an accounting firm, and you want to be an accountant, then you can write a very direct Summary statement without difficulty. If you're in that situation, use a Summary. On the other hand, the more the type of job you're seeking is aspirational because your work experience doesn't directly tie to the type of job you want, then an Objective statement is best. Or, choose an Objective to state your goals if your skills tell your story rather than the work experience you've had so far in your life. The difference is subtle, but every little bit counts when you're trying to stand out and make a good impression.

Each one—an Objective or Summary statement— does the same job of saying what you want to do and why that choice makes so much sense for you given your skills and experiences. It sets the narrative for how you want to be viewed by employers. A strong Objective or Summary statement makes the case, supported by the rest of your resume, for why any company would be foolish not to add you to its team.

The best way to craft your own special Objective or Summary statement is have a written version of your elevator pitch in one window on your computer screen, and Google on the other to look for example Objective and Summary statements on the Web. The variety is endless, so you should pick constructions you like and piece together one that is uniquely your own.

Keywords

I've mentioned the sad truth that your resume will more than likely be read first by a computer instead of a person. Companies use a type of software called an applicant tracking system that reads and scores your resume based on certain criteria including keywords. Given that, the word choices you make on your resume—every single one of them—has extra import in today's world. That works really well if you're a Computer Science major and your resume indicates you know how to code in React and other JavaScript libraries. It doesn't take much discipline for you to remember to include those keywords, and it's easy for someone to ask a computer to find applicants with those terms on a resume. But what about skills that aren't so black and white? That's where word choice in your resume becomes critical to getting past that unforgiving computer's initial screening.

A good starting point for the words you're well served to use in your resume is reading job descriptions for the type of work you're looking for. Find those words that best reflect your expertise and experiences, and find places on your resume where they fit. This runs from basic items that you may not even think of—such as proficiency in the Microsoft Office suite including Word, Powerpoint, and Excel—to more specific terms such as "drive," "creativity," or "problem-solving." Also, many companies list their core values on their website, which are also good sources of traits you know you want to emphasize on your resume. Companies typically take their core values very seriously, particularly in the People or Human Resources teams where the company's recruiters work. They're charged with finding new hires who fit the company culture, which is a very amorphous thing to determine, so companies with core values listed on their website will typically try to screen for people who exhibit those traits. There's no better way to do that than to incorporate those core value terms into your resume where applicable.

It's also a good idea to have a mix of general and specific terms in your resume to capture a broad range of words that a computer—or sometimes even a recruiter—may scan for. For example, as mentioned, many companies like to hire college athletes because of traits such as competitiveness, determination and coachability. A basketball player would be well-served to include broad and specific terms related to her experiences on the hardwood, such as "Division 1 athlete, two-year starter on the conference champion women's basketball team." That's good because it includes a broad term (athlete) and two specific ones (champion and basketball), all of which might be chosen search terms by a computer or human screener looking for competitive traits. Someone with a very different background might add both broad and specific terms in a statement about campus activities, such as "Campus leader who served as sports editor of school newspaper and fraternity rush chairman," which contains a broader term (leader) and specific ones (newspaper, fraternity and rush chairman) that recruiters may be looking for.

Also, don't overlook keywords that relate to experience and ability to excel in a remote setting. Add Zoom, WebEx, or Google Talk—as appropriate—to your list of computer software skills. Find a place for keywords like 'virtual' and 'remote' and note items that were executed remotely, e.g. presenting your internship findings to company management. Employers want to be sure that new employees can thrive remotely, whether or not it's called for at the time you're being hired.

Versioning

I've mentioned a few ways in which your resume can be customized, either by the type of job you're seeking or even the individual company you're targeting. Creating different versions of your resume is a terrific discipline to develop, but you don't need to go overboard with it. I suggest you have one base resume which can serve you for an entire job search cycle, such as when you're seeking an internship as a rising senior or looking for your first full-time job after graduation. That can be fine, but you'll also benefit by making very small tweaks to your resume as you learn more about jobs or companies that capture your interest. For example, if reading a job description gives you an idea for a small word change for your resume, do it. Or if looking at a company's website prompts another thought of a simple word edit to your resume, go ahead and make the update. You'll find that these mini-tweaks to your resume become your new base version for all future jobs. These little tweaks are a good way to keep polishing your resume to make it better and better over time.

About the only situation that calls for having two very different versions of your resume is when you're seeking two very different types of jobs or companies at the same time. Let's say you can't decide between a job on Wall Street or working for a non-profit. My first reaction would be to suggest you review your *ikigai* work and think harder about what you really want to do. But if you were still truly torn and wanted to explore career opportunities in each of those very different sectors, then I'd suggest you create two resumes—one for each potential opportunity. That way, you can emphasize all of your Wall Street traits in one resume, and your non-profit chops in the other. You're describing the same person and the same lifetime of accomplishments to date, of course, but emphasizing different strengths, skills, and experiences to showcase your fit for each on separate resumes. Better to create two purpose-built resumes than try to jam the profile for each into a single document. That would be bad product marketing.

CHAPTER 6 EXERCISE

☐ Write your resume and share it with at least two
friends, someone from your career center and
ideally someone from the industry you're targeting.
Take all feedback with an open mind. Edit and
rewrite actively.

CHAPTER 7

WHERE TO LOOK

Of course, to get a job or an internship, you'll have to find one first. There are several great resources for finding internships, centering on your campus career center and a few key online resources.

Career centers are the strongest bridge from your time in college to the career world after graduation— a bounty of resources to help you at every step along your career preparation journey. Companies looking to hire your school's graduates work with your career center to arrange visits to job fairs, receptions, and on-campus interview schedules. Career center counselors can help you choose a career that's a match for you, and to find internships or other experiential learning opportunities on campus, as well as with companies who have an established interest in your college's students and graduates. But too many students don't avail themselves of the resources in their career centers. Someone should write one of those sappy love songs about campus career centers, because they're so ready to love and have so much to offer, but they're too often ignored. Still, like the proverbial forgotten lover, their loyalty remains strong and they're always there when you need them.

Since your campus career center is the liaison between employers and students at your school, you should start familiarizing yourself with your career center and its programs from the moment you step on campus. They're eager to hear from you right away, and nothing would chafe them more than not hearing from you until you're a senior ready to graduate. Every employer interested in hiring from your school will be routed through your career center, so they have all the information about who's coming to campus to meet students. The career center's activities start early in the fall. While you're still unpacking your bags and sprucing up your dorm room after a summer away from school, the career center has already set much of its calendar. So it's in your interest to check in at your campus career center early each school year to review what's already been scheduled, and check for updates throughout the school year. The calendar shows which companies are coming to campus, and what events and activities have been scheduled. Most importantly, you want to be sure you're aware of when the actual interviews are scheduled, so you don't miss out on getting the chance to get interview slots secured with the companies and opportunities that interest you the most.

Online Resources

In addition to the career center, there are a bevy of online resources that list internships and entry-level job opportunities. You should seek them out often. In fact, I encourage you to make it a daily habit because it requires so little investment of time to passively stay aware of new opportunities, but has a huge payback to know about those newly posted jobs as soon as they appear online. Just as it should be nightmarish to think about the perfect employer who visited your campus without you knowing about it, it should make you shudder to think that the perfect job for you was posted and then filled without you ever having seen it. You can't start too soon. It takes very little effort to set up alerts on the major job sites to notify you—via email or notification on your phone - when there's a new posting that's right for you. Best of all, these alerts are free.

Your school probably has partnered with Handshake.com, which boasts relationships with more than 900 colleges and universities as well as a half-million employers. With numbers like that, it's the 500-pound gorilla of college recruitment, and the number-one resource for job opportunities on campus, internships, and full-time hiring for your school's graduates. There are two other resources not to overlook, which aren't affiliated with your school but are well-known to employers, and will be your go-to resources after you've graduated. Of those, my overall favorite is LinkedIn—especially for entry-level jobs. LinkedIn is the hub of modern recruitment for most industries, so a huge number of jobs are posted there. It's not quite as good for internships, although many internships are listed on LinkedIn. My second favorite general site is Indeed.com, which is different because Indeed harvests jobs from thousands of employers' websites and lists them all on Indeed.com's website. Just like on Handshake, you can set up multiple alerts on LinkedIn and Indeed.com to get regular notifications about new jobs, paired with tools that make it easy to apply for those opportunities and attach your stored resume and cover letter. There are also several specialty sites for internships, such as Internships.com and CollegeGrad.com, which do a great job of gathering internship opportunities in many industries and locations.

I strongly suggest that you visit all these sites regularly, and register to get alerts for new roles posted as they appear daily. You may feel that the emails or alerts on your phone are spammy or intrusive, and fret that many of the jobs in the alerts don't precisely match what you're looking for. But I urge patience here. Just get into the habit of taking the minute or two a day to skim the alerts to find the jobs that matter, and ignore the ones that don't interest you. Also, don't over-specify in your searches on the mistaken assumption that you'll only see perfect-fit jobs. That's a lazy fantasy. If you need to skim through a few clunkers to find something great, it's worth it and only takes a few extra seconds to do the sifting. More important, you don't want to miss out on job listings that could be great fits for you because you've tried to be surgically precise in crafting your job alerts. There's no such thing as the perfect alert that only tells you about dream jobs. What a tragedy it would be if a great job for you got filtered out and you never saw it. It's human nature that job posters thinking about the same job will write their job listings using different words, or check different boxes while posting it. Better to see a few extra jobs you can ignore, rather than being overly precise about your search criteria and missing out on a bunch of relevant jobs that are expressed a little bit differently than you expect. If need be, you can always adjust the alert so you get a better selection of job listings to review.

Applying in Volume

I'm also a believer that applying for jobs is a volume game, so you've got to apply to a lot of jobs. Kiss a lot of frogs, you might say.

In today's online world, the marginal effort to apply to a new job is miniscule. Your resume, even if you want to make a few tweaks for different roles, will speak for itself. Many online applications don't even allow for a cover letter. Given that the effort is de minimis, the emotional commitment you associate with any one job application should be minimal, too. You should have a fairly low bar to decide whether to apply. When in doubt, apply, because otherwise it's a sign you're thinking too much about the choice. Apply now, consider whether you're committed to the job later. In truth, the job listing itself doesn't provide enough information for you to know if it's a great fit or not. You can't see the intangibles such as working for a great boss, what opportunities you can have, and more. There's plenty of time in the interview process to find this out. So for the most part, get your resume out there and get on with your day.

For some jobs that you apply to, however, you'll be very excited. It will seem like a perfect fit. You'll feel yourself getting stoked about the job already. Those are the ones that are worth additional effort. Craft a unique cover letter for these if the application accepts one. After you apply online, figure out if anyone you know can introduce you to someone at the company. I'll have more to say about this when I discuss networking later in this book. When the job looks great, you need extra effort to assure that you'll stand out and can have your application reviewed by a real human being and not just a bot in the company's applicant tracking system.

There's another path that has nothing to do with your career center, and doesn't wind through the online job sites. It's what recruiting pros call the hidden job market—the jobs that you only learn about by your own exploratory efforts, or when companies reach out to you with opportunities that aren't advertised anywhere. You may be forced to explore the hidden job market if you've got a very specific interest that's not likely to be filled by the companies that visit your campus, or even listed on the mainstream job sites. In most cases, your ability to access the hidden job market will be based solely on the effort you apply to it via research and networking.

Be creative and proactive about how to network.

For example, if you're interested in interior design work, go visit local showrooms or design centers and strike up conversations with the owners. You'll be surprised how many people love speaking with students interested in what they do.

Whether through your career center, the job sites, or by following clues on your own while you search the hidden job market, you'll want to cast a wide net and go through the mental exercise of considering a variety of opportunities—kind of like the career equivalent of trying on clothing for size.

Joe Calamusa, who heads a program at the University of Alabama that prepares students for entry-level sales roles at major corporations, says he coaches his students to be "offer collectors" and keep an open mind while they learn about companies. An example of his: a job at an industrial distributor that might not catch your eye at first might be a better fit for you than doing marketing for a professional football team. "Sign up for every interview you think you might even potentially consider one day," Calamusa said. "Go interview. Study and prepare for the interview. You don't know what you don't know. Let them sell you on them."

Bear in mind that there's a huge difference between collecting offers (which can be good) and accepting offers from more than one company (which is terribly, terribly bad). Some students accept multiple offers, or casually renege on offers they've already accepted. That's an abhorrent practice which will not only reflect negatively on you, but will also stain your school's reputation with that company and damage chances of future candidates from your school. It's a little like asking several dates to the prom, and then choosing just one at the last minute—except it's much worse than that. Don't do it. I emphasize it here because I know it happens too much already, and I know how much it annoys the recruiters who work so hard to attract talent to their organizations.

CHAPTER 7 EXERCISE

☐ Set up daily alerts on Handshake, LinkedIn, and
  Indeed.com. Get used to receiving daily alerts, and
  develop the habit of quickly scanning them to see
  if there are new jobs that catch your eye. Experts
  say it takes 21 days to develop a new habit, so you'll
  be an expert at quickly scanning alerts in no time.
  It's a habit you'll be well-served to keep throughout
  your career.

CHAPTER 8

INTERVIEWING

He might have been one of the worst candidates I had ever interviewed, but I came close to making him an offer anyway. Let's call him Ralph. On paper, Ralph had some—but certainly not all—of the background I was looking for. It was barely enough to qualify for an in-person interview. There was one job on his resume that I thought could be germane to succeeding in the role that was open, but that turned out to be quite different than it seemed. Ralph was not particularly dynamic or interesting. His eye contact was infrequent and fleeting. He rambled, and frequently missed the point of what I was asking about. In sum, the gas meter over Ralph's shoulder was pinned near Empty for the majority of our session.

Still, there was just one thing that went right, but it was an important one. When he first sat down at the interview, Ralph pulled a thick stack of paper from his briefcase and placed it on the table next to his notepad. He didn't mention what it was at first, but later in our meeting he said it was my company's 10-Q, a quarterly summary of business performance that all public companies are required to submit to the Securities and Exchange Commission. He had read the whole thing, and he'd prepared some questions for me about it. I was impressed. Indeed, I was extremely impressed. But not impressed enough to move forward. I sent Ralph a 'thank you, but no thanks' email a few days later.

Why was this a troubling choice for me? After all, this particular candidate was overall a dud. Still, Ralph had caught my attention because he was so well prepared. And incredibly to me, in this age when the Internet makes it near effortless to get ready for an interview, the vast majority of candidates are barely prepared when they sit for one. So any degree of preparation appears extraordinary compared to the masses of less ready candidates who interview for new jobs every day.

The paradox is that it's so easy, in very little time invested, to be so well prepared for interviews that you'll stand out as an exceptional candidate. Here are the keys to how to prepare for an interview in a way that will set you apart from almost every other person who applies for that job. And it will only take you—at most—30 minutes to prepare for an interview once you get the hang of it. That's the very definition of a half-hour well spent.

Network

You've heard the cliché: it's not what you know, it's who you know. Like most clichés, there's a grain of truth and the rest is oversimplified. Look, let's be honest, you had better know a lot. But who you know matters, too. A personal connection, however slight, can make the difference between being considered, and perhaps also chosen, versus being entirely overlooked.

The biggest mistake I see people of all ages make is to be too reluctant to seek out professional connections. For many of us, our natural inclination is to avoid approaching people we don't know—especially when our goal is something that's beneficial just to us. To many of us, that feels awkward. Or it feels like it's somehow cheating to find success in some way other than entirely on our own. But let me state this clearly: any reluctance of this sort is misguided. In fact, the opposite is true: developing strong networking skills is an essential part of professional success in any field, at any point in your career. So you'll be well served to start getting comfortable with it as early as possible.

Sadly, there is a gender difference about networking that needs to end. A 2018 LinkedIn study found that women are 26% less likely than men to ask for a referral from someone they know at the company where they're applying. Companies absolutely love to get referrals for new hires from their employees. It's not only pre-vetting to get great new employees on board, but it's great for morale and employee retention. LinkedIn's research did not delve into the reasons for the gender disparity, but the clear message is that no one should be reluctant to network aggressively as a foundational career management tactic.

I think the reason for this misplaced disinclination to network is simple: we tend to try to manage business relationships in the same way we manage the types of relationships we're far more familiar with—friends and family. But while some professional connections are based on friends and family, they're still fundamentally distinct and therefore should be managed very differently. Business relationships aren't there whether you like it or not (like family), or only there if you really like the person and want to hang out together (like friends). Instead, business relationships are based on professional respect, shared work interests, personal style, and workplace performance. Sure, it's great if you like your professional contacts personally, and there's no harm in adding a professional component to a friendship or family relationship. But for the most part it's stifling to conflate all those relationship types into one and treat them all the same.

There are two simple rules I like to apply to any attempt to open a business relationship. The first is called 'give to get:' always offer to give some kind of value in exchange for trying to get some something from a business contact. What you 'give' can take many forms. For example, you might offer to give an update on how students are viewing a particular industry or market trend impacting their employment prospects, or an assessment of the company's products—if applicable—to young adults. The second rule is to remember that business contacts are people, too, so being complimentary and gracious go a long way toward making a favorable first impression and encouraging someone to give you some of their time.

"Flattery goes a long way," advises Mary O'Keefe, a vice president and creative director at the Atlanta office of mega advertising agency BBDO, where she runs the creative internship program. "It's a matter of reaching out—a small note of adding something personal to your outreach so that they know this person actually knows who they're reaching out to, and this isn't just a form email. Mention something they actually did in their career and why you liked it. Generally, a personal outreach will get a personal response."

DJ Washington of The Athlete Network is a big fan of what's called an informational interview—the type that's explicitly not a meeting about a particular job, but instead for the student to ask questions and learn more about a particular field or company.

"Identify three to five people and reach out to them. Take the non-aggressive approach," Washington told me. "You're not looking for a job right then and there. Don't worry that there may be no openings now. Just simply say you'd like to learn more about what they do in their role because it's an area you're interested in. You kind of play to their ego a little bit. Most of the time, even if a person feels they can't be of help, they'll offer to introduce you to someone. It's a good way to open the door to future opportunities."

The good news these days is that networking can begin and end with LinkedIn for almost any career you're pursuing. First, you should have a LinkedIn profile and you should amass as many LinkedIn contacts as you can among people you know and people they know. Start with your friends; connect with them. Find people you've worked with in every job you've ever had, as well as executives at any of those companies who you may have had only passing interactions with, and connect with them. Find friends of your parents, and parents of your friends—especially those who work in fields you're interested in—and connect with them. Set a goal to graduate with at least 200 to 300 contacts from all those sources.

Whenever you attempt to connect with someone, LinkedIn's web version (not mobile as of this writing) provides the option to add a brief note of up to 300 characters with your connection request. Always add a note. It's a way to give the recipient a reason to connect with you—even if you're just saying you're their daughter's best friend. Failing to add a note will just look like spam.

There are a few reasons that LinkedIn is so important. Most critically, you can expect that most potential employers will look up your LInkedIn profile and check out your connections. If you had an impressive-sounding internship, they'll look to see who you connected with at that company as a measure of your level of interactions inside the company. If you connected with executives, and people outside the department you were working in, they'll assume that you were active and engaged during your internship experience. On the other hand, if you connected with no one, they may question whether you even had the job. That's bad, even if they can confirm that you were indeed there. Get in the habit of seeking to connect on LinkedIn with virtually everyone you meet in a professional setting.

But the best thing you can get from a large network of contacts on LinkedIn is the ability to find people who already work at a company on your target list of potential employers. You may know someone who works there, or know someone who has a LinkedIn connection there. You can then seek out an introduction to that person to get an insider's take on the company and the role. In some cases, if you're lucky, they may know the hiring manager and be able to put in a good word for you.

If you are connected to someone at the company, that's best of all. If one or more of your connections is connected to someone at the company, that's almost as good. In either case, your goal is to reach a person at the company and get some information that you can share during your interview. It may be in the form of a question, or just to note during the interview that you took the effort to reach out to someone at the company to learn more. That's an example of a small piece of effort that displays your above-average interest in the company, and recruiters and hiring managers love to see that.

Your approach in either case—reaching out to a connection who works at the company, or a connection who knows someone at the company—is quite similar. Be humble, grateful and specific about your objective. For example, here's what you might write via a LinkedIn message to someone you know at a target company.

"Hi Bill. I wanted to let you know that I'll be interviewing at Acme Corp. next week for an entry-level sales role. I'm really excited about it and hope I can connect with you for a 15-minute phone call before then to learn a little more about your company. Please let me know a few times that work for you before my interview on the 25th of this month. Thanks!"

Or let's say your LinkedIn connection doesn't work at the company, but is connected to someone who does work there. In this case, what you're looking for is what's called a 'double opt in' introduction. That means that you and the person you want to meet have expressed, through an intermediary, that you're both open to be connected. So you might write a note to your LinkedIn connection that looks something like this:

"Hi Bill. I wanted to let you know that I'll be interviewing at Acme Corp. next week for an entry-level sales role. I'm really excited about it and I see that you're connected to John Brown at Acme. If that's someone you're comfortable reaching out to, I'd greatly appreciate an introduction. I'd love to connect with John for a 15-minute phone call before my interview on the 25th of this month. Please let me know. Thanks!"

When you get a meeting with your contact, or your contact's contact, your goal is to get their insider's take on the company and—ideally—the role you're applying for. What's the biggest news at the company in the past year? Who are their major competitors? Have there been any changes in the department you'd be working in? What is the typical career path for people who are successful in the role you're applying for? Does this person know the decision-makers for your role, and can he/she put in a good word for you?

The insider's take is very valuable to you for a few reasons. You're looking for clues for whether this is a company that's a good fit for you: do the entry-level roles and career path represent a fit for what you think you want to do in your first jobs out of college? Equally important, you're looking for tidbits that you can bring with you to your interview: evidence that you did the research, things from your experience that you want to be sure to emphasize in the interview, and what questions you'll prepare to ask the interviewer. More on preparing those questions later in this chapter.

Research

Research to prepare for job interviews used to be a chore. Then came the Internet, and now it's remarkably easy. Yet most people looking for a job—not just students—do a poor job of pre-interview research. There's no good excuse for it. They show up for an interview without even a basic idea of what the company does, let alone much about how it's doing. It's a huge missed opportunity because it's the perfect combination of something that's easy to do and yet still a powerful way to stand out from other applicants.

I can teach you how to do background research for any interview in just 30 minutes, if not much shorter. In a pinch, you could even use these techniques to research the company on your phone in the time it takes to ride an elevator up to the office where your interviewer is waiting—but I don't recommend that! As with the tidbits you gather via networking, the benefit of researching the company is that you'll get a sense of whether the job and company are for you, and you'll impress the interviewer with the effort you've taken to prepare via your comments and questions during the interview.

Here's a checklist of what to look for when researching, and why it takes just 30 minutes. Predictably, most of it centers on Google.

1) Google the company name, find the company's website and read the 'About Us' section. This provides a basic overview of what the company does. Imagine that you'll be asked, "Tell me about what we do," and be ready to give a succinct description. Yes, that's a very typical interview question to test for preparation.

2) Google the company name and click on the 'News' tab. See what's been written about it in the past six months, e.g. announcements, and articles written about the company. You'll want to know what's been happening there lately so you can tailor your elevator pitch to account for elements of your own experience that relate to what the company is doing.

3) Google the company name and 'competitors,' then add some of the competitor names to your search along with the company name. You're looking for content that compares the major players in an industry segment, which will tell you how the company you're speaking with stacks up against its significant foes. This is also great fodder for the questions you'll prepare. For example, you might say you noticed that the company has just announced a major new product, or a rival has done the same, and ask how the new product is impacting competition in their industry.

4) Google the names of the people you're interviewing with. At minimum, you'll find their LinkedIn profiles, but you may get lucky and find a news article or company announcement that mentions them specifically. That's a gold mine opportunity to frame a question around a favorable mention of your interviewer in the news, or something in their LinkedIn profile that interests you.

5) Skim the company's website to see if there are mentions of company values, and think of specific stories from your life that relate to how you exhibited those values in your own life. Recruiters love to ask what they call 'behavioral questions,' which means they generally start with "Tell me about a time when ...." Often, these questions relate to the company's values. For example, a frequent company value is integrity, so an interviewer might ask you to describe a time when you saw something you knew was wrong and did something about it.

6) Finally, an item that does not involve Google. If you've been given a job description, read it carefully. It tells you exactly what the company is looking for, and provides hints for what to highlight from your own background during the interview. Bear in mind that the job description describes what recruiters call the "ideal candidate profile," which too often translates as 'human beings not found in nature.' In other words, the ideal profile is indeed ideal, and odds are they won't find someone with every bit of what's in the ideal profile. One huge mistake candidates make is to focus on the characteristics in the job description that they don't have, rather than the ones that they do have. Don't fall in that trap. Concentrate on what makes you qualified and be prepared to talk about that. If it's concluded that your background isn't a sufficient match for the role, let that be their decision, not yours.

7) One last item: for an on-site interview, make sure you know how to travel there and how long it will take for the time of day your interview is scheduled. Then plan your travel time to arrive 20-30 minutes early so you don't have to worry about being late—which leaves an extremely bad impression when it happens. That's one hidden benefit of virtual interviewing from home: you're less likely to be late because of traffic!

That's it, at a minimum. If that sounds like a lot, it's not. Once you get some practice at this sort of research, you'll see that 30 minutes is more than enough time to do this prep work, and you'll be able to get it done in much less time. Of course, like anything we do online, it's easy to follow a trail from article to article and drag on with this research for hours, but that's neither necessary nor called for—and ultimately does more harm than good. You want to be facile at doing this research quickly so that it's not too taxing to prepare for any one interview, and you can interview with many companies and still feel like it doesn't take up all your time or sap all your energy. Efficiency is key. Time management counts.

Questions, including the 'Question Sandwich'

Great questions win the interview. They're the powerful end result of preparing well, and putting all the networking and research you've done into action. Like all the topics covered in this book, very few people do this well, but it's easy to do with some practice. By preparing great questions, you show the interviewer that you have taken the time to learn about the company, you demonstrate your interest in the most powerful way, and you position yourself as a winning candidate. Great questions set you apart and create a lasting impression in the mind of the interviewer. When you don't have questions prepared, interviewers notice.

"Far and away my biggest pet peeve is a lack of questions. Don't come without any questions," said Greene of Northwestern Mutual. "It tells you if they thought about this or they didn't." When you arrive with good questions prepared, "it shows excitement.

It shows me you're paying attention and are engaged in the process."

Questions are at the core of your interview game plan—the objectives and talking points you decide are most important to weave into the interview. You did all this preparation, and the interview is the only opportunity to show it. Almost all interviews conclude with the interviewer asking whether you've got any questions, but you don't want to wait until then. The quicker you get into asking questions, the better. It makes the interviewer more engaged, and assures that you get into the topics you want to talk about.

My favorite technique for questions is one that I developed myself, which I call the 'Question Sandwich.' The point of the Question Sandwich is to use your questions strategically to steer the conversation to a planned talking point. Just as a sandwich has three parts—two pieces of bread plus a filling—the Question Sandwich has three parts as well.

Here's my recipe for a delicious Question Sandwich:

- **Part 1: The Question.** The Question Sandwich starts with a question that you can ask at any point in the interview—not just at the end. It's a question drawn from the data collection in your research and networking. Example: *In preparing for our meeting, I read about the new product that you've launched. I'm curious: what was it in your market research that prompted the company to launch this new product?*

- **Part 2: The Answer.** Because you've prepared a good question, interviewers will generally take their time to provide a thoughtful answer. But in most ways, the answer to the question doesn't matter, because your whole reason for asking the question is to get to your follow-up, which is the next step. In fact, you can use the time that the interviewer is answering as a helpful mental break during the interview. You still need to listen intently, but your mind doesn't need to work terribly hard because you already know what's coming next: the follow-up.

- **Part 3: The Follow-up.** Irrespective of what the interviewer has said in answering your question, your follow-up will almost always be the same: it's the talking point you prepared—the tasty filling of your Question Sandwich. You listen, nod, maintain eye contact and then bridge to your talking point. Example: *"That's very interesting. In my internship last summer, I got to see the market research that the company did to support a new product of its own. It was really interesting to me, and gave me great background for my Marketing Research class during my senior year. I'd love to be involved in creating and interpreting market research in my career moving forward."*

Slam. Dunk.

The beauty of the Question Sandwich is it almost always doesn't matter what the interviewer's answer was during Part 2. In this example, the interviewer might have described extensive research, or that there had been no research at all, or might have said he didn't know the answer. It doesn't matter. The key is the question leads to a powerful talking point and scores points during the interview.

The key to why the Sandwich Question is so powerful is that it's strategic. Its purpose is less about the interviewer's answer and more about your follow-up. That's the key concept to embrace, because it's the difference between boring interview questions and ones that help you get the job. In this way, interview questions can be less about the actual information you want to get, and more a part of your interview strategy to make the points you want to make. The mistake too many candidates make is coming up with bad questions that are not only boring, but provide no strategic benefit to generating interest in you as a candidate.

Boring questions are ones that just provide data that you can safely learn later, or you could have found out on your own via simple research. They don't help the interviewer decide if you're right for the job. Here are a few examples of boring questions: *How many people are on your team? Do you have office perqs like free lunches or company outings? Will the company reimburse me for my cell phone bill?*

Worse still, asking boring questions could signal to the interviewer that you're a poor culture fit for the job. I call these self-immolating questions—the ones that can set ablaze and burn down an otherwise tranquil and pleasant interview. For example, a popular question recommended by some job-search pundits today is, "Can you tell me about work-life balance at your company?" This might be the worst question of all time, but it's quite common anyway. Sure, you might want to know whether your boss is going to be emailing you at night and demanding work around the clock. But in the context of an interview, it doesn't get you any closer to landing the job—and may actually cost you the offer. You can find out about company culture in other ways, such as Glassdoor reviews.

My advice is to be purposeful in preparing your questions. Plan them strategically. Make them less about collecting random facts, and more of a device to tell your story about why you're the best product—I mean, person—for the job. And when you've prepared such wonderfully strategic questions, write them down on what I call your "H Page".

Your H-Page

Once you've done all this great prep work, you want to be sure that the interviewer knows you've prepared and aren't just extraordinarily nimble about making things up on the spot. You also want to make sure not to forget all your talking points. For both purposes, I recommend you prepare a cheat sheet on an actual sheet of paper—not just in a file on your phone or tablet. Place it in a portfolio or file folder and pull it out when you sit down to start the interview. It's not important that the interviewer can read the words on the page; only you need to see it well enough to read it. But the visible proof of preparation is very important, and will set you apart from other candidates who leave the opposite impression that they didn't prepare at all. Don't let them wonder whether you're really good at improv or if you've actually prepared. Visual evidence of preparation leaves no doubt, and separates you as one of the few candidates who has done solid planning for the interview.

I refer to the one-page cheat sheet as your "H-Page" because you start by placing your sheet of paper in landscape mode and drawing a large 'H' that fills the entire sheet of paper. Then turning the paper 90 degrees back to portrait, you see that you've got a top section, a left and right middle section, and a bottom section. You'll fill in each of those sections as you build your H-Page.

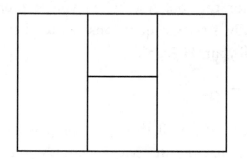

A starting H-page in landscape mode

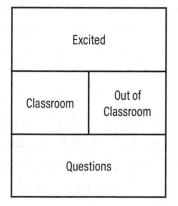

Sections of an H-page

The top section starts with one word: Excited. The word 'excited' is the most powerful word in interviewing. You want to say you're excited about the opportunity that you're there to discuss in the interview, with a few reasons why. It must be sincere, of course, but it also can't be left unsaid. The interviewer needs to be assured that you're indeed excited about the prospect of working in this role at his or her company. So say so. The top section provides a reminder to use the word 'excited' early and often in your interview. The worst fear interviewers have is that you're a great candidate who is not very interested in working for their company. To the interviewer, that's frustrating and a waste of time. Don't leave them wondering whether you're interested in the role; instead, tell them you're excited. Add some notes to yourself as to why you're excited, how it's a great fit, and what has sparked your interest based on the job description and your research. The top section on your H-Page will give you the best chance of remembering to say so, with the reasons why.

The middle sections are where you highlight the relevant parts of your experiences that relate to the job opportunity you're there to talk about—classroom experiences on the left, and all other experiences on the right. On the left side, write the classes you've taken that are most relevant to the job. On the right side, note any activities, jobs and internships, or personal experiences that you've had. Write down the names of anyone you've networked with who works at the company, too.

The bottom section is where you write your questions. Leave lots of room for this because you should come to the interview with at least five rock-solid questions. Write down your Question Sandwiches, including the points you want to bring up in your follow-up.

Overall, the H-Page technique is a great way to keep your talking points in order as you're moving through your interview. It's hard enough to concentrate on answering questions well without having to remember all the things you wanted to be sure to say. The H-Page assures you stay on point regardless of where the interview goes. And having any page leaves a great impression.

Types of Interviewers

You've prepared, your H-Page is set, you've got some strategic, research-based questions ready to go, including a few Sandwich questions. But as the boxer Mike Tyson once said, "Everybody has a plan until they get punched in the mouth." That means you need to be ready to adjust when you walk into the room because you don't know exactly what you're going to encounter. The great thing about being prepared, though, is that you increase the odds of being able to adjust on the fly. When you're prepared, you may be knocked off balance a few times, but you'll always be able to get back on track by remembering your game plan and getting back to your talking points.

One of the best ways to adjust your tactics in an interview is to recognize the type of interviewer you're sitting down with—or speaking with by phone or video chat. It's easy to tell fairly quickly who you're dealing with, and to modify your game plan accordingly. I think the types of interviewers you encounter fit into three basic categories: the unprepared interviewer, the structured interviewer, and the 'entertain me' interviewer. You'll take a slightly different tack with each one.

Unprepared Interviewers are easy to spot. It's obvious right away that they have barely looked at your resume, if at all. They may not even have read the job description for the position you're there to talk about. The Unprepared interviewer generally apologizes at first for not having had time to prepare. It's easy to feel slighted or insulted when encountering the Unprepared Interviewer. After all, you've taken the time to prepare and you might expect a commensurate level of care in preparing by your interviewer, if only as a professional courtesy. But Unprepared Interviewers are in fact a blessing; their unpreparedness is your gain. That's because the less prepared your interviewer is, the easier it is for you to take charge of the interview, get to all your talking points, and impress the interviewer with how prepared you are—not to mention reducing the interviewer's stress over how to fill the 30 to 60 minutes that's been allotted to your meeting.

The Unprepared Interviewer is most likely to start the interview with a very open-ended question, such as the standard "Tell me about yourself" opening that you've already prepared for with your elevator pitch. That gives you the opportunity to set the tone for the meeting from the jump, and even get into some of your questions very early in the conversation. With the Unprepared Interviewer, it's much easier for you to follow your game plan, and to talk about what you want to talk about. Very seldom will you find yourself in a position of getting coldcocked by a probing, unanticipated question jab.

The Structured Interviewer is the opposite of unprepared. These interviewers have a script of common questions they ask of every candidate they meet. In truth, it's the most sensible way for an interview to go, because interviewers can easily compare your answers to the very same questions that have been asked of everyone they've met—possibly over many years. As such, they can easily benchmark your responses vs. the untold number of others who have answered that question before. The key is this type of interviewer has a plan, sticks to the plan, and gives you as the candidate very little chance to take the conversation in the way you want. With the structured interviewer, you'll be working at their pace, not yours. You'll need to strike a balance between answering the questions but getting to your agenda of the experiences you planned to highlight.

With the Structured Interviewer, it's very likely that only a few minutes at the end of your meeting—if that much—will be reserved for your questions. That poses a challenge, because you don't want those terrific questions to go to waste. With the Structured Interviewer, you need to assume that you'll have a chance to ask just one question, if that. So your challenge is to weave those questions into the conversation as part of your answers to the interviewer's questions. The best way to do this is to bridge from one of your answers directly to one of your prepared questions: answer the interviewer's question first, and then ask a question of your own. For example, let's say an interviewer might ask you to recall a time when you overcame adversity to succeed in something. Your answer could start with a personal story of a family crisis, or a failure that you turned into a victory. As you near the conclusion to that story, you might recall one of your prepared questions and segue to it. "When I was researching your company, I was really interested to learn how it overcame some adversity too—how its new product didn't sell well until it made a few changes after launch. I'm curious: what were the keys to making those adjustments, and were you involved in that project?" That's a great way to think about getting to your talking points even if the interviewer takes a very structured approach and dominates your conversation. And it may be one of the only ways you can squeeze in evidence of all your preparation.

The 'Entertain me' interviewer is a variation of the Unprepared style, but without the apologies. This interviewer is deliberately unprepared, and counts on you to carry the conversation. Often, this type of interviewer is applying the 'beer test' or the 'cross country airplane' test, as in, "Is this someone I'd like to have a beer with?" or "Is this someone I'd want to be seated next to on a cross-country flight?" For them, it's all about personal compatibility. Candidly, it's a lazy tactic and doesn't answer much about your fitness for the role. It answers just one question for the interviewer that's barely useful to the company's vetting process: is this someone I'd like to hang out with? But despite its flaws from the company's standpoint, the 'Entertain me' interview is a great one for you as a candidate because—as with the Unprepared interviewer—you have a great chance to set the agenda for the discussion. Unlike either of the other two interviewer types, the 'Entertain me' interviewer also opens up the greatest opportunity to show more of your personality. You can be more free to add appropriate humor, ask and answer questions in more personal ways, and overall form a connection with the interviewer that's not as possible with the frenetic unprepared interviewer or the focused Structured interviewer.

No matter the type of interviewer, some basics are always true. Answer all questions directly and succinctly. No answer should be more than 90 seconds at maximum before stopping. Be comfortable taking a brief pause to form your thoughts. Consider whether the question offers an opportunity to get into one of your talking points, and if so be sure to use that as part of your answer.

Practice

All your preparation will go to waste if you don't take the time to practice for interviews. You don't need to do a full-dress rehearsal for every single interview, but you need to practice the stump speech you will take to multiple interviews so it sounds smooth and natural. You can practice by yourself in front of a mirror or with a friend. You can practice online or in person. In fact, you should practice both online and in person because you'll probably have interviews in both settings. You'll be amazed how strong an interviewing muscle you can build in a relatively short period of time.

Video practice is especially important, and not just because so much interviewing is taking place online after the coronavirus pandemic outbreak. Some companies utilize online interviewing platforms that require you to answer questions on video prompted only by text on a web page—not a live human being who's participating in the interview in real time. SAS, the data analysis and visualization software company, uses a popular platform called HireVue to screen its internship and entry-level job candidates. Students log into the HireVue platform, get prompts for questions, and answer via the camera on their computers. It can feel strange to record video without live feedback, but it's easy to practice on your own just by recording a Zoom of yourself. For the best practice, have a friend compose a few questions for you that you'll see for the first time once you've got your solo Zoom session started. Have fun with it, but use the practice to get used to thinking quickly while forming short, powerful answers on your computer's video camera.

For any video interview, whether it's the asynchronous sort like HireVue or one with a real person chatting with you in real time, remember that you can make a connection via eye contact—even through your computer screen. There's a simple trick for this: be sure to look as closely as you can to the tiny green light at the top of your computer monitor that turns on when the video camera is activated. By looking at the green light, you're looking straight into the camera, and directly into the eyes of the person you're speaking with. To keep it natural, adjust your screen so that the window displaying the person you're speaking with is positioned at the top center of the screen, so looking into the interviewer's eyes is close to looking at the green light, and you'll create the appearance of maintaining eye contact. Before learning this tip, I liked to have two windows on my computer screen—my notes on the left and the video screen on my right. But I didn't realize that when I was looking to my right to make eye contact with the image on my screen, it looked on camera like I was looking away. By aligning the video with the top center, you can more naturally make eye contact with the image on the screen and also be making actual eye contact via the video camera. You'll make better eye contact, and appear more at ease and personal, when you make good eye contact. (Note: Never do a video interview on your phone, unless you can stabilize it using a dock so it stays perfectly still. Nobody wants to see shaky, jarring video—especially when you want the interviewer focused only on you with no distractions.)

To practice for live interviews in particular, it's a good idea to record your practice sessions using the Gallery view. To still be able to look straight into the camera to maintain eye contact, slide the video chat window to position the head of the person you're speaking as close as possible to the top-center of your computer screen. Using gallery view, you'll be able to see what you look like—and sound like—when you're reviewing the recording. You'll be able to see yourself for the full interview—not just when you're speaking. Study your facial expressions when you're listening, as well as when you're speaking. You may find bad habits you want to work out of your routine, such as wandering eyes, looking away, or slouching posture. Every bit of body language is important, so you want to make your best non-verbal impression in addition to all the great things you have to say. What you look like is as important as what you sound like. This type of practice will serve you well for video and in-person interviews.

Of course, what you say and how you say it is important, too. When you review the recording, listen for things you may not notice about yourself in normal conversation. Do you use too many umms and ahhs, do you look away when you're thinking, do you take too long to get to a point or ramble a bit while you're getting into the groove of your answer? All of these are negatives that, with awareness and practice, you can eliminate from your interview repertoire. Practice really does make perfect. Even though it may be excruciating to watch and listen to yourself speak, it's a pain worth enduring. It's normal to hate to watch yourself on film. But improvement can happen very quickly when you work on specific things and review your progress using recorded video.

A crisp elevator pitch is the most important item to master when reviewing yourself on video. It's your main selling piece, and must be practiced so that it can be delivered naturally, succinctly, and with command. You also want to get very good at weaving in a few of your more powerful experiences into your answers as specific examples. Interviewers love examples, and are quick to get frustrated with only general platitudes. With practice, you'll find that the experiences you want to highlight are easy to use as examples that fit your answer to many different questions.

"These kids record themselves on Tik Tok every day, and their videos are short and concise and you know what they're trying to say," said BBDO's O'Keefe. "I think that's a skill set that will probably help them."

Above all, practice so that you leave no doubt that you have prepared. "It's not very flattering to be speaking to someone who feels like they didn't need to prepare," O'Keefe added. "If you're winging it, if it's loosey-goosey, you might still do fine but it doesn't inspire a lot of confidence."

Thank You Notes

Call me old fashioned. No, I mean it, say it out loud: "OK, boomer, you're old fashioned!" I'm used to it, but I also know what works. And while it may feel to you like something from the era of a Dickens novel, writing thank-you notes can be an extremely important and highly differentiating aspect of interviewing and job hunting. The reason is rooted in your eye roll at this very moment (admit it!): it's that so few people write thank-you notes these days. But listen to yourself: the best way to stand out is to do the things that others don't. Writing thank-you notes falls into that category. It's a nice touch to your product.

Like all my advice, a thank-you note is purposeful, not just perfunctory. Sure, just writing a thank-you at all will make you stand out. But the best way for you to utilize a thank-you note is with a specific purpose in mind. It could act as a do-over for a portion of the interview that didn't play out as well as you wanted. Perhaps you didn't like your answer to a question and you remembered the perfect anecdote to tell while on the way home after the interview was over. Your thank-you note is the perfect environment to smooth over that bump. You'll simply use part of your brief thank-you to mention that you thought of a great example to answer that question and write a very brief synopsis of the experience you wish you'd thought of in real time. Thank-you notes are also great to hammer home a point that resonated well in an interview, such as including a link to an article you mentioned, or to underscore a common interest that surfaced in your meeting.

You'll stand out from the pack by writing a brief email—no, I won't make you write a handwritten note—with the following elements:

- Thanks for being generous with your time.

- That you particularly enjoyed a given portion of the conversation, noting the specifics.

- How excited you are for any planned next steps in the process (or just about the topics discussed in an informational interview).

- Any follow-up thoughts, including patch-up work for a question you wished you had answered differently.

CHAPTER 8 EXERCISES

☐ Create your LinkedIn profile, if you don't already have one, and invite as many professional contacts as you can. These can include your friends (particularly those who have strong internship or other professional work experience), colleagues and executives at companies you've worked in, family members and friends of your family—particularly those who work in industries or disciplines you're exploring for your own career.

☐ Pretend you have an upcoming interview, do a practice 30-minute company research project related to a specific role, and prepare an H-Page for that interview, including two to three Question Sandwiches.

☐ Do two mock video interviews with a friend who asks you the same questions in each session. The first interview is a practice round. Review the first interview recording with your 'interviewer,' and identify areas for improvement. Focus on those improvement items in the second interview and review that one, too. Keep practicing and get better.

CHAPTER 9

OFFERS (AND REJECTIONS)

All your preparation pays off when you start getting offers from employers to join their companies for internships or full-time roles. Your hard work is validated. You've gained all the appropriate experiences, done a good job of marketing yourself as a distinctive product, and one or more employers have seen enough potential in you to want to add you to their teams. Congratulations! And welcome to the next phase of your career management challenge, which is what you do after you get an offer. Some of you will love it; you'll accept, pop the Champagne (or sparkling water), feel relief, and anxiously await the start of your internship or new job with high hopes. But others of you may find the post-offer stage as stressful—or even more angst-ridden—as the job search itself.

Why might getting an offer be a stressor and not just time to run a victory lap? There are many reasons. For one, unlike when you applied to college, job offers don't all cluster around the same timeframe in the middle of April. Nor do they have a common date when you must decide, as you did when you finalized your choice of which school to attend. With jobs, you probably won't have all your options neatly laid out for you in the same timeframe. For another, you'll probably need to continue your discussion with companies—past the point of the offer—about topics like compensation and start timing. All that can be stressful.

You'll probably also have to deal with some amount of rejection, which can be the most unsettling of all because you won't always be able to understand why you were offered at one company but rejected by another. It's a time when even the most stoic person's emotions burn hot. In sum, there's a lot still to deal with, even after you've gotten one or more job offers. Let's unpack these issues one at a time.

Timing

As discussed earlier in this book, the recruiting season stretches out through several months of the school year, concentrated in the Spring, but the decision process when you get a job offer may be on a tighter timeline. After making you an offer, employers reasonably would like to know quickly if you're willing to join them. They may ask that you make a commitment before you have all the information you might ideally wish to have regarding potential opportunities elsewhere. You'll gain extra credibility with these employers by being transparent with them about the job discussions you're having with other companies who are interested in you. Be humble but open about how you're thinking about making a decision, decide on a timeline that will work for you, and ask if it's agreeable to them. They may reasonably insist on you making a decision sooner than you'd like, because they'll need to keep looking if you choose not to join them, or you may find that they're willing to work with you.

Let's invoke our mythical friend Paul again to walk through a hypothetical scenario. We'll say that in early April of his senior year, Paul receives an offer for a full-time job that starts during the summer after graduation. Paul is excited about the opportunity, and the company has given him a written offer asking that he respond within a few days. But at the same time, Paul has already had a second interview with another company that he likes, too, and he knows that the other company won't make its offer decision until early May. Paul has a choice. He can jump to the 'bird in the hand' approach and accept the offer he's got, but that's not always the best way to play his hand. In most cases, Paul is better off engaging both companies in his dilemma: ask the company that's made him an offer if it can extend his deadline, and also ask the other company if it's possible that their process can be expedited. Such a request may be denied, but it's at least a fair discussion to have. Companies most often want candidates to be comfortable with their decision, so Paul is working with high odds that he'll get some consideration by humbly, gracefully, and transparently sharing the facts of his situation and requesting some consideration. He'll be sure to tell each company how grateful he is to have advanced in their interview process, and how excited he is about the prospect of working there. He'll learn more about the companies with this approach, too. If they're too inflexible, it might be a clue to the company's culture that Paul can factor into his decision.

Working around timing issues can surely be stressful. But remember: in Paul's hypothetical situation above, he had an offer from one company and was progressing in his discussion with the other, so both companies obviously like him a lot. He's also showing a degree of professionalism for how he's handling the situation: being open, and explaining his reasoning and decision process. Plus there's the non-trivial part of it that's just for Paul: he wants to feel good about his choice, and he has every right to feel he's made his decision with the most possible information at hand.

There are plenty of wrong ways to handle this type of situation, too. For example, some might see Paul's scenario as having an easy out: just go ahead and accept the offer in hand, still stay in the second company's process, and make a final decision only after the second company has made its choice. But I find that approach to be unseemly and disingenuous, and certainly unprofessional. I'll leave it to the ethicists to determine if it's unethical, too, but at minimum the scales are tipped that way. It will certainly tarnish the school's reputation with the jilted employer, and possibly your own personal brand as well.

I'm also not a believer, in most cases, in proactively pitting two competing companies against one another in an attempt to create a bidding war for your services. If you're a sports fan, you may fancy yourself as akin to a star professional athlete in free agency, collecting bids from competing teams and driving up your price. But when applied to one's first job after college, that analogy breaks down for a straightforward reason: leverage. While the star athlete has leverage, and can demand that one team out-bid another to win his signature on a new contract, you as a college student or recent grad are far less likely to have sufficient leverage to play this game. By the forces of supply and demand, there's simply way more supply for you than the star professional athlete, which translates into diminished leverage for you. If you overplay your hand, you risk losing one or both options, and that's a poor risk-reward tradeoff. Even if you're that rare student who has substantial leverage in the job market, because of exceptional and rare skills or pedigree, then you'll be better served in the long run to act humbly and negotiate fairly.

All of which brings us to the proper way to negotiate an offer.

Negotiating

Recognizing that you're not likely to have much leverage, most employers aren't put off by an attempt to negotiate terms of an offer. Many expect it. As long as you act professionally, you should be able to engage in a discussion about how flexible the company can be in the terms of your initial offer. Negotiating won't always be successful; offers won't always be improved via negotiation. Especially at the very large companies like Big Four accounting firms, and others who annually hire hundreds to thousands of interns and new college grads, offers are fairly standardized so room for negotiation is likely to be thin. But it's worth a try. When you're just starting out, every little bit of extra financial boost is helpful. Plus, when you conduct yourself maturely and professionally, it most often will reaffirm to the employer that they've made a good choice in extending an offer in the first place.

Two keys matter most when negotiating an offer: be fact-based, and be consistent. Your school most likely compiles anonymized salary data showing what other students earn, sliced by industry and geography. There are several online resources as well such as Comparably, Salary.com, Glassdoor and PayScale. The various data sources almost certainly won't agree, but collectively they'll give you a good sense of the range of pay that's reasonable for any job you're considering. It's more than fair to ask for more if you're at the low end of the range, or under it. Also, there are lots of levers to compensation, not just base salary. Your total compensation might include a performance or sign-on bonus, or moving expenses. For full-time roles, but not internships, it's commonplace for technology companies and some others to also offer stock options as part of a compensation package. Develop your fact-based strategy and don't change or add anything as you progress through the negotiation. You don't want to 'move the goalposts,' as it's called, by adding to your target compensation request midway in the discussion.

Early in my own career, I had a very successful negotiation in my first job after getting an MBA. I went to work on the business side of a newspaper—not at all the most lucrative career path for new MBAs. In fact, most media jobs at the time offered well below-average starting salaries compared to classmates entering fields like investment banking and consulting. Still, I did my homework and took what I thought was an eminently reasonable position: I told the newspaper that my goal was only that my starting salary meet the average for a graduate of my school, and provided evidence of what that meant using data from my business school's career center. Of course, I knew that average for my school was well above the average for my chosen industry. Still, my argument sounded so reasonable—just wanting to be average—that I was able to negotiate a much higher salary than was contained in my initial offer. It worked because I was humble and grateful, brought facts and took a sensible position based on those facts, and I quickly accepted—no moving of the goalposts—when they adjusted their offer to exactly what I had requested. Mind you, in this case, I had a little bit of leverage because I was a known quantity, having had a successful internship the prior summer. Still, it's a good case in point for how a properly conducted negotiation can be successful.

Emotions

None of this, sadly, is easy on the emotions. Sure, there's the excitement of the journey, the vistas of possibility that can be fun to explore, and the exhilaration of actually getting an offer for a dream job. But there's also another set of emotions to battle. The primary one of those is rejection. Some companies will decline to make you an offer to join them. Let's cozy up to that reality, acknowledge its presence, give it a hug and a pat on the head, and move along. The reality of rejection is not going away, but it doesn't get to beat us down, either. Maddeningly, you may find no rationality in which companies are dying to have you vs. which ones swiftly reject your candidacy. There's no job-search equivalent of a 'safety school' as when you were applying to college. The real world doesn't work as neatly as that.

When you get rejected, take stock. Reflect on all the steps you took to prepare and how you performed. Assess for yourself where you did well and where you think you faltered. You may have been a star throughout the process and just fell victim to a numbers game. Alternately, you might have made a fatal error—or a few of them—that you can learn from and be sure to eliminate from your interactions with other companies in the future. Did you prepare as well as you could? Did you fumble on an interview answer that you knew you should have been prepared for? Did you sufficiently and credibly communicate your excitement about the opportunity? Review the 'game tape' in your memory with an open mind to how you could have improved. Only through your own reflection, and ability to be constructive with yourself, will you learn enough from a rejection to improve yourself and be a better job candidate in the future. As life skills go, candid reflection is a pretty good one to focus on. Pick yourself up, learn a lesson or two to help you improve yourself, and move on. There will be plenty more victories than defeats in your future.

Even getting an offer can have an emotional toll in this manic time. The start of one's career is all about limitless possibilities, and finding your true passions, yet it's often difficult to switch from all that plethora of options to just the one job you've chosen. Sometimes it's hard not to focus on all the great things you won't get to do, instead of the one thing you now get to do based on the job offer you've accepted. It's all natural and normal, and carries its own miniature grieving process. Choosing a job can be a bit of a letdown. Most of the time, though, that letdown is temporary. If you've followed the steps in this book, building from your *ikigai* throughout the process, then you will have chosen a career start that's right for you. Go celebrate and enjoy! Odds are you're in a great spot.

Sometimes, though, students find themselves feeling significant remorse. It might be simple cold feet and second-guessing, or it might be that they simply made a choice too soon. Sometimes, an offer finally comes for a job you really wanted, but you'd written off that opportunity because you hadn't heard from the company in so long. Getting that kind of news can make you question whether the job you've already accepted is the wrong one to take. That situation creates a very troubling dilemma. It would be a very big step to renege on an offer you've already accepted, and take a job with a different company. Companies hate it, and it will make your career center nervous too because it could hurt the school's relationship with that employer. But your primary responsibility is to yourself, so that's the tiebreaker in a situation like this. Many of my career center and employer friends will not like to read this, but it's the right choice to renege on an offer in certain—albeit rare—situations.

I'll share one more story from my past that illustrates my point of view on when it's OK to renege on an offer. It happened in April of my junior year in college—on my birthday, of all days. I remember it to this day as the worst birthday I ever had. Weeks earlier, I had accepted a summer job that I was very excited about, and thought would be a terrific addition to my resume. I was to be a summer associate at The Associated Press (AP) bureau at Rockefeller Center in New York City. That summer was certain to be an exciting one, because the Democratic National Convention was being held in New York's Madison Square Garden. It was hinted I might even get a press badge to visit the convention floor, repping the AP. Most of the summer, though, promised only observational value—being around the newsroom operation and performing odd jobs, but only being close to the journalism and not participating in it. Still, I was excited and looking forward to it.

But then came my birthday, when I got word of another option that I'd previously written off. After hearing nothing about the opportunity for months, I was offered a summer reporter job at The Herald Statesman newspaper in Yonkers, N.Y. While it hardly carried the marquee value of the AP job, it was a chance to be an actual newspaper reporter. In my mind, it was a far better opportunity to develop my skills and have 'clips'—copies of stories published in the paper under my byline, which are the currency by which reporters display their abilities to editors to get hired in the future. It was vexing, but I felt my choice was clear. So I accepted the Yonkers job and called my contact at the AP directly, told him that I was sorry, but explained my reasoning. Thankfully, he told me it was a good choice and not to worry about it. I think the candor and humility I expressed on that call worked, because two years later the very same AP contact helped me get my start as a full-time journalist when I joined the AP bureau in Miami.

My conclusion: reneging in that case was OK, but it was excruciating. That could be the best guide you'll have for when it's OK: how painful it is. If it's extraordinarily hard to do, but you own up to it and be honest with yourself and the individuals at the companies involved, then it's probably the right choice for you. Just don't do it a lot. I've never done it again.

CHAPTER 10

ON THE JOB

Congratulations. You've gotten the offer, accepted, agreed on a start date, and now you've shown up for your first day on the job as an intern or a full-time employee. In the Covid-era world, that first day may be a series of video calls from home. But if you're lucky, you'll be flesh-and-blood in an actual workplace sitting with your new colleagues. As the new person, you're the one that your new co-workers are anxious to welcome, but also the one they're trying to quickly size up to learn who you are. Do you come off as entitled, over-confident, and above it all? Or do you go out of your way to be courteous, humble, and eager to learn? First impressions count, and you'll want to position yourself as early as possible as someone who wants to help, does any task that's needed, is ready to understand the business, and willing to work hard while being a pleasant and productive member of a team.

Your job is Job One. Understand your assignments, ask questions and do your best work. Do what's asked of you and more. Complete every task as if it's a reflection of you, and bears your signature, whether it represents a great challenge or isn't particularly fulfilling in the moment. Make every assignment a high-effort exercise, even if it doesn't excite you at first.

The first impressions you leave on your teammates can win you advocates or skeptics in a hurry. Experienced people in business notice a standout employee very early based on their habits—even in the first few hours the new hire is in the office. The best ones are noticeable. "On the first day they introduce themselves, walk around and shake hands, and express their enthusiasm," said BBDO's O'Keefe. "Then, throughout their time at the agency, it's wonderful when interns are hand raisers. They'll circulate if they don't have a lot going on and ask people if there's something they can help with." And while not required, it's always noticed when interns offer to stay late when the full-time team is on deadline and could use extra help. "It's really nice when they lean in that way," O'Keefe says. "That's when they're going to get some really good experience as well."

When I was growing up, my father used to tell me stories of something similar. One of his first jobs after graduating from journalism school was at the United Press bureau in Pittsburgh. He found that the best way to learn was after hours, too. But instead of working late, those lessons were over drinks, late into the night with his more seasoned colleagues, at their 'clubhouse'—a bar across the street from the office. I'm not necessarily recommending regular drinking to learn the ropes, but learning any way you can is always a good idea.

Your Powers of Observation

In addition to doing your job well, and beyond your assignments, you want to be as observant as you can be. Watch what's going on around you. Take not just mental notes, but real written notes, of all your observations. What seems odd? What practices don't make sense? What seems like it could be done better? Write it all down—privately and for your eyes only. You may think 'I'm sure there's a reason they do it that way,' and there may be a good reason. But that doesn't mean it can't be done better. It's important to start taking notes right away because your impressions are still pure, and aren't yet polluted by knowing all the reasons why things are as they are. Keep a file on your computer, or notes in a notebook that you keep in your desk drawer, of all these first impressions that you gather during the first couple of weeks on the job—no longer. Then pull out those notes after you've been at the company for a couple of months. You'll see that most of the things on your list are things that actually can be improved, and things that should change, and you can start to recommend adjustments that will make the job run more smoothly, add more value to your customers, or generally help the business thrive. That's your job as an employee at any level: help the business prosper.

When you've come up with ideas for how to improve things, you need to research and communicate those ideas in a professional manner. Your opinions are interesting, but the case you make for change needs to be more than just your opinion. You need facts, data, rationale—not just opinions. There's an expression in business called "HiPPO", which is an acronym for 'highest paid person's opinion.' You're probably not yet the highest paid person, so your opinion won't win the day all on its own. But data can trump opinion—even the HiPPO's take—so you'll want to figure out how to show data to support your opinion about things. For example, you might notice a process you believe is entirely inefficient, and therefore is costing more money than it should and creating a poor experience for customers. You could measure the time it takes to get the process done using the current process, and experiment with a new process to see how much more efficient you can make it. Always keep your boss informed of your ideas and thoughts of how to fix them, and gain approval for spending work time on researching solutions. By being appropriately humble but energetic, you can get your boss and your colleagues engaged in the process of helping you implement ideas for improvement. Be sure to always complete the assignments you're given before devoting time to your ideas for improvement. That's a great recipe for success in any environment.

When you have an idea and facts to support it, flesh it out and present it in writing. Remember when they used to tell you in math class that getting the right answer wasn't enough, but you also had to show your work? It's the same in the workplace. Always show the logic of your thinking, and be sure to bring facts and available data. As with your job interviews, you want to erase any doubt that you haven't thought things through and aren't just good at improvising on the spot. "It's ideal to have something written down and some kind of sketch to represent it, even if it's just a stick figure," advises BBDO's O'Keefe. "Bringing something visual to represent the thing that you're going to make is a really good skill to repeat."

I got some good advice early in my career: you're interviewing for your next job every day. That means that your day-to-day performance in your job is your best daily contribution to your own advancement. It's simple: do a great job, be a terrific team member and teammate, lift the performance of the entire team by pitching in wherever you can, and help make the team perform better. Always provide a basis for your opinions, always bring a potential answer when you cite a problem that needs to be solved. Be constructive, polite, and direct.

You can also fast-track your learning by asking yourself 'What would I do?' when observing managers and executives at your company when they're faced with a problem to address. It could be something commonplace such as 'How would I have answered that question?' to something more foundational, like 'Should we as a company be focusing as we are, or should we be focusing on something different?' You'll grow faster as a professional when you've given yourself this role-playing experience, so that when you're sitting in a bigger chair you'll already have been practicing for it for a while. When you're consistently observant, when you role-play, when you ask 'What would I do?' or 'What would I say?' and when you become an active participant in making your department or your company better, you're positioning yourself for future success. Actively seek out ways to always be learning.

In any case, think about what the company needs and do it. Be vigilant about looking for ways to try to be helpful, and don't be too proud to help out even in menial ways. Every contribution matters. But also be thinking about how the experiences you're gathering will be useful to you for the ways you want to build a foundation for your career. Do what you can to assure that you have the experience you want—one that will give you talking points to take to your next interview cycle.

Above all, have fun. Especially for interns, you'll never have another immersive opportunity to dive into a company for just ten weeks or so and really get to understand the business, the people, and how they do things. You'll learn to recognize company culture, too, which will be very important to evaluating companies that have a culture that's right for you. Are people robotic or creative, do people feel empowered or ignored, is there evidence of advancement or do people look stagnated, are you impressed by your co-workers' intellect and drive or does it look like people are just going through the motions to get their jobs done? Getting skilled at recognizing these and other key workplace traits will be a key to you finding environments that suit you and allow you to thrive throughout your professional career.

CHAPTER 11

ONGOING CAREER MANAGEMENT

The coaching points and recommendations in this book are meant to get you launched. They're about getting you started on a trajectory toward fulfillment and success, by your definition of each. But your start is just the first set of steps in a long, exciting journey. That path is likely to take many turns as you move through your life. You may set yourself on a course that defines your lifetime from the start, or you may take a first job out of college that has nothing to do with what even your second job will be, let alone your life's work. No matter what, you should plan on a lifetime of collecting experiences, enriching yourself by challenging your comfort zone, and expanding your knowledge and abilities. Keep refining your *ikigai*—not just with career in mind, but for every facet of your existence. By continuing to be reflective about the lessons in this book, you'll get better and better at defining new vectors for the straight lines that you'll draw through your experiences to point to the next thing you want to do in your professional and personal lives. There's always a reason, based on your experiences, that forms the straight line to something new and exciting. Or at the very least, it's easier to make transitions when you can draw a straight line toward it.

Most of this book is about getting a job and building a career. Implicit in that is working for other people. But what about starting a business and working just for yourself? Good news: all the same lessons apply. As an entrepreneur, your resume is the pitch deck. Your interview is the investor meeting. Your product is still you, but it's also the product itself that your budding enterprise is building.

If that future path is entrepreneurship—starting a company of your own—it will be the hardest thing you've ever done, and perhaps the most exciting and satisfying, too. There are, of course, many successful people in the world who have started multiple companies and never worked for anyone else. They're often heroes in our society, and their celebrity is warranted. They represent the American Dream. But I would always recommend working for someone else for a few years before starting a business on your own. Better to be paid to learn the basics of business than to have to learn everything on your own, one mistake at a time. That's no slight; as humans, we all make mistakes. By extension, all businesses make mistakes too, because they're populated by humans. But if you bring a level of focus, awareness, and purposefulness to your time working for someone else, then you'll have a much greater chance for success when you set out on your own. You'll still err and learn. Mistakes are a great teacher. Even celebrity entrepreneurs, who are heroes and heroines in our culture, make mistakes. Often, they're colossal ones. But you can increase your chances of entrepreneurial success by learning from your mistakes on someone else's dime. And then stride out on your own and start the company that nobody else could.

Still, we aren't all entrepreneurs. Most of us don't have the mix of guile, audacity, and unwavering confidence in a dream that all true entrepreneurs have. This isn't a character flaw or some sort of inherent weakness. It's just a fact of who we are or who we're not—a piece of self-awareness, if you will. If there's an entrepreneur inside you, let it out. If there's not, then there are plenty of other pathways in life that will lead you to happiness and the best person you can be.

Be it on an entrepreneurial path or not, the lifetime skills discussed here are ones you'll continue to sharpen and improve. They will enable you to find the most rewarding journey that's a match for you and the livelihood and lifestyle you want to create for yourself. You'll always be improving your product, even as you change how you position yourself as you move along in your professional life. It just takes an occasional deep reflection to reset yourself, decide on adjustments to your plan, if any, and forge ahead. That's what your own career planning is all about: a deliberate plan that you build one experience at a time, like laying so many bricks one on top of the other to build a solid, impressive wall. That's what managing your career—and life—are all about.

Remember the career competencies discussed earlier in this book? One of those competencies—an important trait that employers are looking for in hiring new college graduates—is career management. Here's how career management is defined in that study:

"Identify and articulate one's skills, strengths, knowledge, and experiences relevant to the position desired and career goals, and identify areas necessary for professional growth. The individual is able to navigate and explore job options, understands and can take the steps necessary to pursue opportunities, and understands how to self-advocate for opportunities in the workplace."

Career management in this context means that employers want new graduates to understand what it takes to develop one's livelihood over time. But as you'll recall, career management was one of the topics where students assessed themselves with far greater scores than employers gave them. In other words, employers generally think that students aren't as good at career management as the students think they are. Take that as a cue that you need to be thoughtful about the investment you must make in a path of continuous self-improvement, which will reflect in your contributions in the workplace—not to mention your impact on society at large.

Never stop launching and relaunching yourself, with reflection on how the experiences of your lifetime will refine and potentially reshape the person you see in yourself. You get to launch as often as you like. I hope this book will help make your first launch a majestic one.

About the Author

Rob Feinstein is a pioneer in the online recruiting industry, a longtime software industry executive, and a former award-winning journalist. Through those experiences, he's gained a unique understanding of the real world of today's technology-driven employment marketplace from a hiring manager's perspective.

He was vice president and general manager of MonsterTRAK, the college recruitment services arm of online jobs giant Monster.com. Prior, he was vice president of products at CareerPath, a consortium of newspaper publishers that combined to form one of the Web's premier job search destinations and—under Feinstein's direction—one of the Web's largest and most deeply searchable resume databases. Through those experiences, he has a deep network of employment industry contacts, particularly from companies who hire the most college graduates and college student interns, and directors of the campus career centers whose job it is to assure their students secure strong starts to their careers.

Feinstein is currently vice president of solution management at BlackLine, a finance controls and automation software solution for corporate accounting departments. He also offers one-on-one career consulting for college students and new college graduates. For information, visit his website at robfeinstein.com.

He holds a Master of Business Administration from the Amos Tuck School of Business at Dartmouth College, a Master of Journalism degree from the Columbia

University Graduate School of Journalism, and a bachelor of History from Brown University. He and his wife, Tara, live in Los Angeles, CA.

Acknowledgements

This book would not have been possible without the generous and insightful help of many friends, colleagues, and family members. I cannot say a hearty enough thank-you to all of you, but I will try.

I'm indebted to the many old and new friends from college career centers and employers who hire college students and new graduates, some of whom I've known for many years, and all of whom were gracious enough to accept my requests to give their time to this project. Your tales from the front lines, and your perspectives, were an invaluable asset to this project. I'm forever and especially grateful to Kelley Bishop, Scott Williams, Sean Treccia, Mary O'Keefe, Kayla Woitkowski, Kaitlin Greene, DJ Washington, Michael Van Grinsven, Will Ruch, Joe Calamusa and Dr. Fran Lawrence.

Several friends who represent potential readers of this book—rising young professionals and their parents—also generously gave their time to read the book's early drafts and offer insights and suggestions. Thank you to Erika Kerekes, Jenny Connelly, Jill Sandin, Pamela Gwyn Kripke, Casey Curtis, and countless others who helped inspire and assist me.

Thank you to Tess McCabe for the book's striking cover and interior designs, to Barbara Davis for her careful and thoughtful editing, and to Diamond Alexander for creating my website at robfeinstein.com.

Thank you to my mother, Eve, who inspires me to this day with her joy of life and positive spirit. Thank you to my late father, Selwyn, a newsman who taught me the value of careful writing and arduous editing.

Thank you to my son, Graydon, who contributed to this book with his stories and creative energies.

Finally, and most importantly, I want to thank my wife, Tara, for always supporting me, instilling confidence in me, and encouraging me to always reach for my best—often beyond what I believed my best could be. I could not have taken on, let alone finished, this project without her. This book is dedicated to her.

CPSIA information can be obtained
at www.ICGtesting.com
Printed in the USA
LVHW082023090221
678835LV00014B/2281

9 781735 537306